A PICTURE IS WORTH
1,000 WORDS

A PICTURE IS WORTH 1,000 WORDS

image-driven story prompts and exercises for writers

by phillip sexton
photos by tricia bateman

WRITER'S DIGEST BOOKS
CINCINNATI, OHIO
WWW.WRITERSDIGEST.COM

A Picture is Worth 1,000 Words. Copyright © 2007 by Phillip Sexton. Manufactured in China. All rights reserved. No other part of this book may be reproduced in any form or by any electronic or mechanical means including information storage and retrieval systems without permission in writing from the publisher, except by a reviewer, who may quote brief passages in a review. Published by Writer's Digest Books, an imprint of F+W Publications, Inc., 4700 East Galbraith Road, Cincinnati, Ohio 45236. (800) 289-0963. First edition.

11 10 09 08 07   5 4 3 2 1

Distributed in Canada by Fraser Direct
100 Armstrong Avenue
Georgetown, ON, Canada L7G 5S4
Tel: (905) 877-4411

Distributed in the U.K. and Europe by David & Charles
Brunel House, Newton Abbot, Devon, TQ12 4PU, England
Tel: (+44) 1626 323200, Fax: (+44) 1626 323319
E-mail: mail@davidandcharles.co.uk

Distributed in Australia by Capricorn Link
P.O. Box 704, Windsor, NSW 2756 Australia
Tel: (02) 4577-3555

Library of Congress Cataloging-in-Publication Data
Sexton, Phillip.
A picture is worth 1,000 words : images, ideas, and exercises for writers
by Phillip Sexton ; photographs by Tricia Bateman. -- 1st ed.
      p. cm.
ISBN-13: 978-1-58297-472-9 (hardcover : alk. paper)
ISBN-10: 1-58297-472-1 (hardcover : alk. paper)
1. Authorship--Problems, exercises, etc. I. Title. II. Title: Picture is worth a thousand words. III. Title: Picture is worth one thousand words.
PN147.S39 2007
808'.02--dc22
                   2006023147

Editor: Amy Schell
Designer: Tricia Bateman
Production Coordinator: Mark Griffin
Photographer: Tricia Bateman

19.99

To Mom and Dad,
for your constant support, encouragement, and love.
There are no better gifts.

PHILLIP

For Mom, who gave me my foundation.
For Dad and Gail, because of their endless faith in me.
For Tommy and Trace, my constant sources of inspiration.

TRICIA

CONTENTS

HOW TO USE THIS BOOK

> " Writing is an exploration.
> You start from nothing and learn as you go. "
>
> —E.L. DOCTOROW

The first sentence of Doctorow's quote always struck me as romantic, acknowledging what I thought I knew about writing. It's an adventure, a journey, that shows me things about myself and the world that I could not

have guessed. And while that's all wonderfully true, it's the second sentence that brings everything crashing back down to reality.

Writers do start with nothing. That's the truth of the job, whether you do it for fun or profit (with very little of that, for most). And it's often that nothingness that most vexes beginning writers. Getting started, finding ideas, and tapping into inspiration so compelling that you can't do anything but write can be difficult.

There are a number of books available that feature writing prompts, each one attempting to provide a temporary solution to the "nothing" that we all must overcome. *A Picture Is Worth 1,000 Words* is quite a bit different.

The pages that follow contain 112 exercises. Each one includes a writing prompt paired with an original photo. The photos are indispensable to completing the prompts, providing clues, visual cues, and

details that you might not otherwise consider when imagining a story or scene. In addition, they add a certain aspect of puzzle solving to the process, forcing you to think about what you're looking at, interpret it in your own way, then utilize those details in your story. This extra level of stimulus and interactivity may be more than you're used to getting from writing exercises, which is kind of the point.

A short discussion related to a specific aspect of the writing craft precedes each exercise. My goal is to get you thinking about how you write, then encourage you to try writing in new ways, using the prompt and photo as your starting point.

I want you to commit to writing a minimum amount for each exercise. At least 1,000 words—approximately two pages. In my experience, real progress—the kind marked by measurably tighter, more efficient, and more powerful prose—only comes from having invested enough time to write 1,000 words or more at a time. Writing a paragraph or two, even if done so religiously, doesn't make much of an impact. That's why I think most writing prompts, while great for motivation, don't often do much to improve your work.

A sample prompt appears on the next page. When you're ready, that's a good one to start with. But keep in mind that you needn't work through these prompts in any particular order. Tackle whichever ones you find most intriguing. Or alternatively, work with the prompts that address the elements of fiction that concern you most.

I believe that writers are visual creatures, inspired and influenced by the images that surround them everyday. The ultimate goal of this book is to help you start finding ideas everywhere you look, on demand. That way, you'll never have to start "from nothing" again.

-Phillip Sexton

INTERPRETATIONS

The wonderful thing about working from photos is that they can be interpreted in so many different ways. We each respond to different visual cues, and those cues shape the story we're inspired to tell. This makes photos a great tool for writing groups and writing workshops, as many different people can work off of the same image, yet create vastly different tales. (Comparing the end results can be particularly fun.)

Throughout this book, you'll come across photos that detail everything from simple settings to complex combinations of story elements. Open yourself up to multiple interpretations, even if it seems like your story choices are limited. This will make working with the photos even more illuminating, while also giving your imagination an excellent workout.

EXERCISE

*Some might see the photo at right as having a limited number of interpretations.
Challenge yourself to think of two entirely different stories, using the image as your setting.
If you find that the exercise helps you develop more imaginative ideas, consider writing
multiple interpretations of every photo prompt.*

BEGINNINGS

"Well begun is half done." —ARISTOTLE

Exactly. The most important part of your story is the beginning. There are three reasons for this. First, if your opening pages fail to captivate, all the effort afforded the middle and the end is wasted energy. The reader simply won't make it that far—and you can't expect them to start where the story does get good, if it's not the beginning. Second, the beginning of your story sets the tone and attitude for everything that follows. It's where your protagonist is introduced and the foundations of your plot built. Finally, it's your one shot at making an impression upon agents and editors.

That said, don't let the importance of your story's beginning intimidate you. You're a writer, which means you have more courage than fear. Relish the challenge. The following exercises will guide you to think about everything from your opening line to that first twist in the plot.

TRICIA L. BATEMAN
8411 ELLISON
CINCINNATI, OH 42526
45226+1205

Your Starter Pistol

In every story there comes a moment when the writer must provide his protagonist with her entrée into the plot. The catalyst, also known as an inciting incident, must be explicit and it must happen relatively early in the story. Readers get bored quickly.

Your protagonist might discover a thief in her office. The thief makes off with information of great value to her. Alternatively, she might receive a surprising e-mail from a forgotten lover. This entrée might be low key—even possible to ignore for a day or two—but eventually your protagonist will have to attend to it.

EXERCISE

Write a scene in which your protagonist receives the letter pictured at left. There's no return address. What's in it? How does your protagonist react to the contents and why?

The Plot Point

Screenplay, by Syd Field, outlines the basic story structure every good tale should have. A key part of this structure is the "plot point," defined as an incident or event, which spins the story in new, unexpected directions. Your first plot point (there can be many) occurs after the inciting incident detailed on p.17. And where the inciting incident serves to indicate where your protagonist enters the plot, the initial plot point is the moment at which their commitment to the story is secured.

In William Peter Blatty's *The Exorcist,* the inciting incident happens about twelve pages in, when Regan's mother, Chris, hears "rats" in the walls for the first time. The first plot point occurs thirty-seven pages later, when Regan's bed begins to shake unnaturally for the first time. The girl also exhibits a personality change. Chris doesn't believe Regan's story about the bed shaking and instead takes the girl to a doctor who diagnoses her as depressed, failing to realize the reality of the sinister forces at work.

EXERCISE

Your protagonist is about to enjoy a balloon ride. Write the scene leading up to the first plot point. What happens that spins your story off in an exciting new direction?

PROLOGUE-JAM

Weigh the benefits and the dangers of a prologue before committing to its use. Consider: 1) It might not be necessary. Can your reader determine the information conveyed in the prologue based on what transpires in the story itself? If so, what do you need a prologue for? You're simply delaying her from getting to the real story. 2) A prologue forces you to start your story twice. It's hard enough to engage a reader once, much less a second time. Why chance losing him?

On the other hand, a prologue can 1) provide readers with a different, possibly illuminating, viewpoint on the events to come in the main story, and 2) infuse your story with tension and excitement well before your main plot might otherwise develop it. If you opt to use a prologue, make sure it contributes critical information that will illuminate your reader's understanding of the main story.

EXERCISE

Imagine a story in which a buried treasure is hidden beneath a bridge. Then, write a prologue detailing the events surrounding the treasure's burial (note the date on the bridge's plaque). When finished, think about how you could relay those same elements to the reader without relying on a prologue.

Real Motivation

Your story begins at a party. Write a scene in which your protagonist decides to pursue the woman behind the glasses. Rather than grounding his motivation in lust, develop a history that adds depth to his motivation and informs the reader as to how he will try to win her over.

What drives your character? What causes him to care about your plot in the first place? I'm not concerned with the explicit motivation imposed by the mechanics of the plot (i.e., hero must stop villain from setting off bomb; father must win back the love of his son; etc.). No, what I'm interested in is what motivates your protagonist *before* the story even begins. What is the psychology or personal history that helps determine his actions?

I've always found that knowing the answer to this question, even if the reader does not, enables the writer to craft a more believable story. The hero must stop the villain from setting off the bomb because of his unwavering commitment to the safety of humanity (most normal people would let the authorities handle everything). The father must win back the love of his son because he himself was once abandoned.

PERFECTION

If you're like me, crafting the opening line of your story can be a frustrating experience. You want it to be perfect, both intriguing and unique, while conveying a rhythm and style that immediately captures reader attention. It also has to illuminate something about the scene being set, character being introduced, or situation taking place. It's the way you introduce yourself to your reader—a bit like shaking hands, in fact. Is your grip weak; palms sweaty? Or is it firm and confident? Keep in mind that this is also the first line an editor or agent will read. Sweating now?

Anytime you begin to write an opening line, ask yourself the following questions: What's the very first thing you want your reader to know—idea, time, place, situation, mood, or character? Why? What's so interesting or important about that specific thing?

EXERCISE

Write an opening scene that takes place at the location pictured. When you're finished, go back and examine the first line, asking the questions detailed above. Does it establish the important elements you wanted it to?

MAKING AN ENTRANCE

A critical part of any story is the reader's introduction to your protagonist (and your antagonist, for that matter). His entrance must be in line with the initial image you want to convey to the reader. For example, in *The Sea Wolf*, by Jack London, Wolf Larsen's entrance is a classic, establishing him as a ferocious, powerful being, less a man than a force of nature. If Larsen's introduction portrayed him pouring a cup of tea in the galley, readers would envision an entirely different character. Likewise, in Leonard Gardner's *Fat City*, protagonist Billy Tully is introduced in the process of moving from one lousy hotel to another. He's a has-been prizefighter, down on his luck, divorced, and borderline alcoholic. The respective entrances of these two men tell readers volumes about their character.

EXERCISE

Write a scene introducing your protagonist (seen at left) to the reader for the first time. What kind of entrance will you give him? Will he be at a particular location or performance? What kind of setting is it? What do your choices say about the character?

High Anxiety

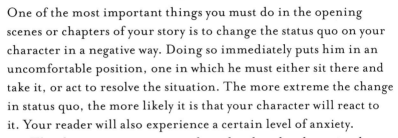

One of the most important things you must do in the opening scenes or chapters of your story is to change the status quo on your character in a negative way. Doing so immediately puts him in an uncomfortable position, one in which he must either sit there and take it, or act to resolve the situation. The more extreme the change in status quo, the more likely it is that your character will react to it. Your reader will also experience a certain level of anxiety.

The change in status quo is also related to the plot point detailed on p. 18. Every time a plot point occurs in your story, it's a sign the status quo has changed as well. It's a moment at which your protagonist must readjust his strategy in order to try and return the status quo to normal (or acceptable) conditions.

EXERCISE

Your protagonist is an alcoholic. His wife has put up with it for many years, but finally she's had enough. Change the status quo on your protagonist. Tell us what happens because of it.

Cut the Fat

Many writers are prone to producing more material than they really need to make their point. I'm guilty of it. You probably are too. Is it because we love our own writing so much, we can't imagine others not feeling the same way? Is it paranoia—the sense that we've not provided enough information to *really* explain how old something looks, or how capable our protagonist is? If so, we're wrong on both counts. It's not how much you write, but how you write.

Your reader is impatient. They want you to get to the point, even if your prose is stunning. If you allow your story to sit there, think about becoming a painter. You have a page, maybe two, to engage your reader. Consider those first few lines an advertisement of sorts. Then think about how quickly you change the channel when an advertisement doesn't get right to the point.

EXERCISE

Write an opening scene in which your protagonist leaves work only to discover that his tire is flat. As he's pulling the spare from his trunk, one of his fellow co-workers, whom he's secretly been attracted to for years, walks up and offers to help out. When you revise it, pay close attention to any information that fails to advance the story. Can it be cut?

NEED TO KNOW

After all this talk about getting to the point, cutting the fat, and crafting the perfect first line, you may be under the impression that every story must begin with action immediately. If so, let me clarify. The initial incident that propels your story forward doesn't have to happen right away. In fact, it probably shouldn't. You have time to establish a sense of place, mood, or an idea of character—but you must do so efficiently.

How much information does your reader need to have before the incident occurs? Must they know certain things about your protagonist in order to make sense of his reaction to the incident? Do they need to understand the layout of a particular setting? Answer questions such as these before you begin to write. Doing so will help focus your opening, even if it runs for several pages.

EXERCISE

Write a scene in which a young student begins her first semester at the local art academy. She will meet someone there who will change her life. Before you begin, think about what information you want the reader to know before she meets this person.

HYPNOSIS

The opening of your story is also the entry ramp that your readers use to disengage from the real world and lose themselves in yours. Think about that as you write those first few pages. Are you establishing a rich, detailed setting, crafting intriguing characters, or delightful exchanges of dialogue? In such moments, you are acting as hypnotist to a willing audience, ushering them into a secret place from which they will ignore both the passage of time and curious observers. Pages dissolve into vivid imaginings and any sense of "reading" falls by the wayside.

When you write, examine your opening pages carefully and ask yourself: Will these words transport my reader? Is there any moment that doesn't ring true, or any line that disturbs the rhythm of my words? Be conscious of these things. They are the finger snap that brings your reader back to reality.

EXERCISE

Write a scene in which a little girl and her father select a pumpkin for Halloween carving. Focus on establishing a realistic relationship between them, as well as a palpable mood. Will your readers lose themselves in this scene?

CHAPTER TWO

DESCRIPTION

"Even in the midst of love-making, writers are working on the description." —MASON COOLEY

Sad to say, but it's probably true. It's the writer's instinctive response to think in terms of how something looks, feels, sounds, and acts. Turn the page and you'll find exercises that will encourage you to experiment with a variety of descriptive techniques, from personification to juxtaposition. You'll also be asked to think about how description can be used to make characters act in certain ways, pushing them around the page.

As this book hopes to inspire you through the use of photographic images, description is your tool for creating images of your own, images that inspire others and create worlds more real than any photo.

Complex Simplicity

Some of the most effective descriptions occur when you imbue relatively simple subjects with vivid characteristics that help to establish mood or a captivating sense of time and place. A sentence or two is all it takes. One of my all-time favorites comes at the beginning of *The God of Small Things*. Author Arundhati Roy sets the mood immediately with a brief two-line description of flies. Yes, flies. She writes: "Dissolute blue bottles hum vacuously in the fruity air. Then they stun themselves against clear window panes and die, fatly baffled in the sun." Notice how carefully her words have been chosen.

Also, be particular about *what* you choose to describe. If there's no reason to do so, then don't. Lengthy, overwrought, or pointless descriptions will bore your reader faster than a dull plot.

EXERCISE

Examine the leather chair shown at right. Write a story in which this chair is used to establish the setting in which an important confrontation occurs. Your description of the chair need not be long, but make sure it conveys a specific, vivid sense of place.

Reduction

There is a descriptive technique that I like to call "reduction," taken from the cooking term, which means to boil down a sauce to increase its richness of flavor and consistency. When reduction is used in writing, an author takes something with many varied elements and "boils it down" into a simple, yet rich, description that conveys the idea of those elements without specifying them. In his wonderful book *Serenity: A Boxing Memoir*, Ralph Wiley provides my favorite example: "Dick Sadler stood out among the old heads. He was a brown leather thumb of a man with deep eyes and a peppering of small moles on the skin beneath them."

I find "brown leather thumb of a man," in particular, to be an extraordinary use of language. Six words that provide so vibrant a description of Sadler that you can intuit his attitude, stance, walk, skin texture, and countless other details. To describe all of these things individually would take paragraphs. Wiley does it in an instant and it works.

The image at left includes many complex elements. Rather than describe them all, use as few words as possible to convey a sense of the bar in its entirety. Use this description in a scene detailing the bartender's efforts to get an attractive waitress's phone number.

Blindfolded

A good writer uses all of his senses to describe physical things. The way they smell, feel, sound, and so on. Even the best writers, however, tend to anchor their descriptions with visual details, adding smells, sounds, and textures as warranted.

It's understandable, of course. For most of us, sight is the main contributor to our perception of the world. We think about things in terms of color, size, and shape. And it's a safe bet that most of us fear losing our sight more than any other sense.

Failing to utilize the full range of her descriptive powers, however, inhibits a writer's ability to render things as richly as possible. Like the muscles of your body, all of them need to be exercised. Make a conscious effort to do this. Try to rely on smell, hearing, touch, and taste more often. Doing so will improve your descriptions immeasurably.

EXERCISE

While exploring his grandfather's farm, a young boy comes face-to-face with a horse for the first time. Write about the encounter, but when you describe the horse, don't use any visual details. Rely upon your other senses.

{ 43 }

DESCRIBING THE INVISIBLE

Description most often focuses upon people or things that can be viewed or places that can be visited. But occasionally, you'll choose to describe something abstract. Typically this takes the form of either a literal description ("February is cold, but, thankfully, the shortest month of the year") or a metaphor of some sort ("February settled upon the land like the black shroud of death"). Because concepts, feelings, and states of mind can be difficult to describe, we typically do so quickly and move on.

EXERCISE

Hone your writing prowess by describing "childhood" without falling back upon specific events or images one might associate with childhood.

Consider the following passage from Tom Robbins' *Jitterbug Perfume*: "[February] is the meanest moon of winter, all the more cruel because it will masquerade as spring, occasionally for hours at a time, only to rip off its mask with a sadistic laugh and spit icicles into every gullible face …."

Robbins describes February for a total of 359 words and each line is poetry. He uses simile, metaphor, personification—every trick in the book, really, to make February a character as much as a concept.

One Inch at a Time

Think about the different ways in which you might describe a particular subject. If it's an object, person, or place, you might hone in on the physical details, describing them either literally or metaphorically. If an action or concept, you might anthropomorphize it.

I recommend that occasionally, as an exercise, you try describing the same subject multiple times. Each attempt should be unique in style and content. Why? Because many writers get locked into description by rote, i.e., they have a favorite way of describing things and they stick to it. It's easier. It's comfortable. It's also lazy.

You want to be better than that, don't you? Put a little extra effort into honing your descriptive powers. Doing so will enable you to vary your writing style, keep your readers on their toes, and discover things about your subject you hadn't even thought of.

EXERCISE

Write four scenes about the inchworm pictured. Each scene should be at least 250 words. Specific descriptive elements or words related to the worm may not be used more than once. In other words, each description must be totally unique.

What's My Motivation?

Writers often fail to consider the extent to which description can drive their story. Characters need motivation for their actions no matter how minor or seemingly inconsequential—everything from opening a door to cooking breakfast. You want them to think, act, or react in a certain way? Description can help get the job done.

Describe a room as being cold, dark, and empty, and your character will be motivated to either turn on a light or exit. If you describe a floor as sticky, your character will either move out of the room or put some shoes on. If he doesn't, that indicates a second, stronger motivation making him stay put. His willingness to ignore the sticky floor enhances the importance of his primary motivation. Bottom line? Make it a habit to think about the way in which tiny descriptive details can influence your characters' actions.

EXERCISE

Your protagonist and her boyfriend have a fight. After nightfall, the power goes out in their apartment, forcing them to light candles. How does the candlelight change the ambiance of the room? How does it influence your characters?

Living, Breathing

Personification takes place when you imbue an object or abstraction with human characteristics. Done well, the descriptions that result can be unusually powerful. Here's an example from William Shakespeare's *Romeo and Juliet*: "Arise, fair sun, and kill the envious moon,/ Who is already sick and pale with grief." Clearly, the human characteristics enhance not only the description of sun and moon, but also the relationship between the two, as well as the mood of the piece overall.

Here's another example, taken from *The Masque of the Red Death* by Edgar Allen Poe: "And now was acknowledged the presence of the Red Death. He had come like a thief in the night. And one by one dropped the revelers in the blood-bedewed halls of their revel, and died each in the despairing posture of his fall." The Red Death is, of course, pestilence, made all the more frightening by the implication that it lives, a thinking, plotting thing.

EXERCISE

Write a scene that takes place in the setting pictured. In it, a wife finally tells her husband she wants a divorce. Use personification as one of your descriptive tools, particularly when detailing the tree shown.

What Dreams May Come

For several hours each night, we dream. Oftentimes, upon waking, we can recall vivid snatches of this dream world, although it may not make much sense. The next time you wake from a dream, immediately write down everything you can remember about it. Don't worry about what was happening, just capture the images you saw. Describe everything. Include as much detail as possible. Many dream images relate to real world concerns. Are any such issues evident in what you recorded?

Although describing such images will seldom, if ever, be necessary to your writing, becoming proficient at rendering bizarre and unusual details might, particularly if you're interested in science fiction, fantasy, or horror. Once you've captured some of your own dream images on paper, try the exercise below.

EXERCISE

After falling asleep, the woman pictured awakens to find herself on the ground in a strange, unreal place. Describe what she sees when she looks up. What happens next? Think about the reasons behind the dream. Remember, the images you describe may reveal something important about her waking life.

Spreading the Wealth

Description is best when delivered in small doses. Far too often, writers begin to describe a complex person, place, or thing, and keep going until there's nothing left to say. It's as if they want to get the description out of the way so they don't have to think about it anymore. Unfortunately, providing so much description at one time kills the plot's momentum, bores the reader silly, and leaves fewer surprises for the rest of the story.

If you've ever been guilty of this, try spreading your description across the entirety of a scene. Or, consider taking even more time to complete it. Your reader will put the pieces together as they go, allowing them to move through your narrative quickly, without having to read a rap sheet on what someone looks like or how they act.

There are many elements in the photo worth describing, including the horse, rider, barn, and weather. Write a scene in which you describe one or each of these elements, but portion out your description amongst action, narrative, and dialogue. Don't let it fall onto the page in one giant clump.

ODD MAN OUT

You have a line-up of suspects. One of them looks totally dissimilar to the others. The witness behind the screen points to the unusual looking suspect and names him guilty—just like in a (bad) movie.

You would never use such a scene in a real story, of course. It's ludicrous. But the idea of juxtaposing one thing against another in order to highlight its unusual nature has merit. In other words, if you really want to make something stick out, describe how it differs compared to the status quo. Film director Tim Burton made good use of such comparisons in *Edward Scissorhands*. In the film, Edward is a freak, trying to survive a nightmare of 1950s suburban perfection. Placing Edward in such a setting heavily accentuates his bizarre nature. Try using this technique in one of your own stories.

EXERCISE

You've moved into a new neighborhood where every house looks similar to the one next to it. At the end of the street, however, you see the house pictured. Describe this house in the context of the others. Who might live in such a house? Why?

CHARACTER

"The business of a novelist is … to create characters first and foremost, and then to set them in the snarl of the human currents of his time…" —JOHN DOS PASSOS

Characters are the great love of writers. If you didn't cherish their thoughts, speech patterns, appearance, and … well … character, you wouldn't bother writing about them in the first place. And, or course, the really wonderful characters do a large part of your job for you, directing you in matters of how they will act, what they will say, and when *they* are finished with your tale.

Over the next few pages you'll experiment with stereotypes, outrageous character types, and a variety of techniques for indicating character without resorting to simply telling the reader what you want them to know.

DRESSED TO IMPRESS

Without saying a word or moving a muscle, your character conveys a massive amount of information about who he is, what he thinks, and what his situation might be, based solely on what he wears and how he wears it.

It's wonderful shorthand for fleshing out the characters you haven't time to fully explore and for underscoring the characteristics of those you do. Consider what the ill-fitted tuxedo says about the man at the dinner party, or the faded blouse implies about the woman at the office. Every scuffed shoe and starched collar provides reams of information for your reader, and makes your job easier.

EXERCISE

Based on the shirt at left, what can you determine about the man who wears it? Write a scene in which you use a description of this shirt to convey personality, status, situation, and attitude. Consider how other characters might react to the man, based on what's implied by your description.

{ 61 }

ACTING UP

Sometimes a character's actions are used to convey who they really are, even if it belies who they appear to be: A timid, middle-aged man is moved to startling action at a moment of crisis. A spontaneous, happy-go-lucky college student works two grueling jobs to pay for school. At the opposite end of the spectrum are those characters whose actions obscure reality: A laughing, laidback boss who takes out his anger at home. An insensitive young boy who craves nothing but affection. Does the act of writing one feel different than the other, i.e., action to reveal character vs. action to obscure character?

EXERCISE

Consider the man at left. Write a scene in which his actions accurately portray his abilities and interests. Then write a scene in which they do not. Is your character a convincing liar? Does he even realize the lie inherent in his actions? Do those around him? How does this enrich the character?

What's My Motivation?

Love. Envy. Fear. Lust. What motivates your protagonist? It can be any number of things but, generally, it's pretty clear what the primary motivation might be. It's good to keep in mind, however, that every character, whether major or minor, is motivated by something. Don't let any character act without taking their motives into account. No one speaks simply to hear his own voice, or to provide the protagonist with useful (i.e., conveniently available) information. Your characters don't live in a vacuum; they all want something.

Rule of thumb: If an encounter between characters is important enough to include in your story, it's important enough to make each and every one of their motives a factor in how the encounter plays out.

EXERCISE

Using the image at left as your starting point, create an encounter between three characters whose motives are at odds with one another. Perhaps two characters will be aligned against one, or maybe all three want something different. Then, introduce a fourth character into the mix whose motivation is totally unrelated to the other three. How does the scene play out, and how did the fourth character's motive affect it?

ACTION!

In the exercise on p. 61, we used clothing to help define our character. Now let's take the opposite approach. Rather than describing your character through her physical appearance, try creating a sense of who she is and how she looks based on what she does and how she moves.

For example, if your character shuffles rather than struts, your reader might readily assume that she's neither a snappy dresser nor in the best physical shape. At the very least, she doesn't carry herself with confidence or pride. Precise word choices, in this case, shuffle versus strut, enable you to convey as much information in a brief sentence as in a hastily composed paragraph.

EXERCISE

Write a scene in which the character at left is confronted by an overbearing neighbor. Convey as much as you can about the woman through a description of her actions rather than her appearance.

LAZY SUSAN

In his best-selling suspense novel *Avenger*, Frederick Forsyth spends the first half of the book building up a large cast of supporting characters so richly detailed that they rival the protagonist for both "screen time" and relevance to the plot. The effect is such that, for a time, one wonders if the protagonist is, in fact, the central character. What this technique really does, however, is provide each character with an airtight, believable motivation that informs how she acts—as well as how she *interacts*—with the protagonist.

Imagine the person in the foreground of the picture at left is your protagonist. Flesh out his history, appearance, and personality traits, assuming that he will be charged with carrying your narrative forward. Now, "rotate" the image left or right, as if the characters were all sitting on a lazy Susan. Bring one of the background characters to the fore. Make this person your "new" protagonist, and develop him just as fully as you did the first.

EXERCISE

Write 1,000 words in which your new protagonist interacts with the original. Does the fact that you envisioned the first character so fully (while assuming his "lead" status) enrich this interaction? Is it easier to write?

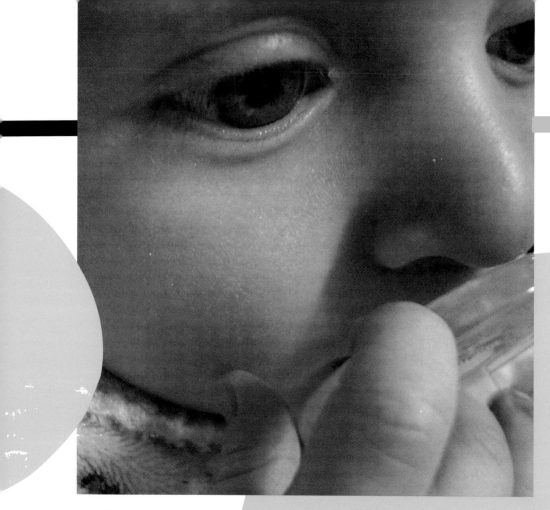

Tabula Rasa

Most character creation begins the same way. A writer fills up a relatively blank slate with generalizations about what the character looks like, how she acts, what motivates her, who she spends time with, etc. Once those initial ideas are determined, more specific details follow, either prior to, or during, the actual writing of the story. Either way, new characters begin life the same way almost every time: newly hatched, a little unsteady, and kind of bleary-eyed. It's only through writing and rewriting that characters finally gain their feet and become as well defined as their authors hoped they would.

But the process could be easier. One technique that helps is to focus on who the character becomes, rather than who they are. Think about what traits your character will have gained and lost by the end of your story and why those changes occurred. Working this out in advance gives you a clearer picture of how (or if) your character evolves and why.

EXERCISE

The infant pictured is only a few months old. Make up the personality traits he will have as an eighteen-year-old. Then, write a scene in which the child exhibits some of these traits for the first time. How do his parents react? How does the boy modify his behavior based on their reactions?

THROUGH THE
LOOKING GLASS

There are three basic cornerstones to character creation: how your character looks, acts, and thinks. A critical part of this last trait is what your character thinks of himself. Those beliefs influence how he reacts to people, and how he interprets their reactions to him. A man who thinks himself dull, for example, might assume that the woman who turns her back to him has grown bored. In reality, she's simply looking for the bathroom.

Real people—and good characters—almost never see themselves as others do. Knowing this aspect of your characters will make them deeper, richer, and easier to write.

EXERCISE

Write a description of the woman seen through the glass. It should reflect what she believes to be the truth. Others may disagree. Once you've finished, write a scene in which she interacts with co-workers, friends, and/or strangers at the bar pictured. How do her beliefs about herself influence the way in which this interaction takes place? Keep these ideas in mind whenever you create a new character.

Stereotype This!

Most writing texts will tell you to avoid stereotypes, with good reason. There are two situations, however, in which they work to your advantage. First, stereotypes act as unspoken shorthand between writer and reader, enabling you to convey basic character traits without explanation. For extremely minor characters, this has some value.

The second use is more important and more fun. Stereotypes suggest a specific set of character traits that can (usually) be counted on. The morbidly obese man gets tired easily. The buff young hero is courageous. The raven-haired Italian beauty is flirtatious. Use such expectations to your advantage by defying them. Your reader will be pleasantly surprised. A word of caution, however: don't try this too often. Eventually, the stereotype that defies expectations becomes its own kind of stereotype, i.e., the foul-mouthed grandmother, the thug with a heart of gold, etc.

METHOD ACTING

The "method acting" technique is one in which an actor tries to tap into any strong personal experiences that might enable him to more closely duplicate the psychological and emotional state of the character he is going to play. If the part is so extreme or specific that he has trouble making the connection, he might try to replicate the living conditions of the character. For example, prior to filming *Saving Private Ryan*, Tom Hanks and his co-stars suffered through a week of boot camp in order to better grasp the brutality of being a World War II soldier.

When you write, think about the emotions at play in each scene. Then think about any personal experiences that closely resemble what your character is going through. Think about your emotional state at the time. If you can't relate because the emotions are too foreign or extreme, consider interviewing or observing someone who shares your character's experience.

EXERCISE

Write a scene in which a waitress is forced to handle the lunch rush alone. At the same time, her boyfriend, the fry cook, begins to argue with her. Chances are you can identify with the heat of an argument. What about the pressures of being a harried waitress? Consider observing one in action. Might doing so help you identify with her, and, consequently, change how you write the scene?

Just Outrageous Enough

Some authors create characters that are so over the top, they approach caricature. And yet, when it's done well, that very same character can become a pop culture legend. It's a hard line to walk, which is why most writers steer clear. A tad too much wacky eccentricity and the reader loses interest.

Consider Ignatius J. Reilly (*A Confederacy of Dunces*), Lionel Essrog (*Motherless Brooklyn*), or six-foot-four transsexual Roberta Muldoon, "a stand out tight end for the Philadelphia Eagles" (*The World According to Garp: A Novel*). All three are particularly unusual, with physical or behavioral characteristics that set them far apart from polite society. And yet, due to the skill of their respective creators, we're willing to believe that such peculiar persons might exist.

EXERCISE

Try your hand at walking the narrow line between creating an icon and a caricature. Using the image at right as your inspiration, craft a story about a truly odd protagonist and see if you can maintain the optimal mix of outrageousness and believability. Once your story is finished, let your "personal trainer" (see the exercise on p. 199) read it. Do they believe?

CHAPTER FOUR

DIALOGUE

> "I learned what I know about writing the hard way. I stubbed my toe over every obstacle there was in the path of the beginning writer. Dialogue got me down and had me almost licked." —ERLE STANLEY GARDNER

It's true. Dialogue will challenge you like nothing else. Who would've imagined that the act of writing words "spoken" by characters could be so difficult? From capturing realistic speech patterns and slang to the high wire act of nailing accents without your characters sounding like sorry stereotypes, dialogue makes life interesting, to say the least.

The exercises that follow challenge you to examine the intonation, emotion, delivery, and rhythm of dialogue. Once you've developed the ear for it, dialogue may become your favorite part of the writing process.

WORD MUSIC

There are a handful of writers who craft dialogue with such style and skill you can't help but smile at the way their characters speak. Think Anna Quindlen, Quentin Tarantino, John Irving, or Preston Sturges. Whether highly stylized or dead on accurate, great dialogue is like great music. You could listen to it for hours.

Unfortunately, most of us aren't nearly so skilled. We're better off limiting our dialogue to brief conversations scattered in amongst lengthy passages of action and narrative. It doesn't have to be that way, but there's a balancing act to be mastered first. Great dialogue can't sound exactly like real speech. Record a conversation sometime, then play it back and you'll see. How dull would your dialogue be if every other word was "um," "uh," or "like"? Real speech isn't nearly as clean as what fiction demands. By the same token, your dialogue must sound natural. After you've written some, read it aloud. Does it sound like something a real person would say?

EXERCISE

The woman at left is obviously very pleased about the topic of conversation.
Write a lengthy scene of dialogue detailing this conversation, making sure to break up the speech
with occasional bits of narrative and movement. Read the story aloud. How does it sound?

The Details of Dialogue

In much the same way a character reveals his true feelings through body language, he can use word choice, intonation, and inflection to reveal them through speech—even if he's saying what another character wants to hear. For example, if your character's girlfriend is accusing him of having an affair, you could write: "I'm not having an affair," he said guiltily.

You could do this, but don't. If you have to use adverbs to describe *how* your character is saying something, it needs to be rewritten. Good dialogue does the work of conveying attitude, emotion, and subtext for you. Using the example above, your character might say: "I'm not having... an affair. No way."

The character's hesitation—and immediate reinforcement of his assertion—implies that he's not telling the truth. No adverbs needed. Get it?

EXERCISE

Write a scene in which one of the characters pictured asks the other several probing questions about a recent trip he or she took. The questions and answers should be phrased in such a way as to indicate the lack of trust between the two characters, without being overt.

Good Dialogue Gone Bad

Good dialogue happens when you streamline real speech to be more reader-friendly and keep it sounding natural at the same time. This is more difficult to do when tempers flare, emotions run wild, and your dialogue needs to sound more impulsive and spontaneous. There's nothing quite so comical as bad dialogue that is screamed or shouted.

When you're writing a confrontation, a confession, or any other scene in which characters may be weeping, yelling, arguing, or debating, be disciplined enough to hold these exchanges to the same high standard as your more deliberate passages.

EXERCISE

Craft an emotionally charged, dialogue-heavy scene, using the subject of the photo as your inspiration. Allow the scene to get as loud and strained as you like, but be sure it meets the standards of good dialogue. Can you imagine someone delivering the words you've written, at an emotional pitch that doesn't sound ridiculous? Act out the scene to see if you're right.

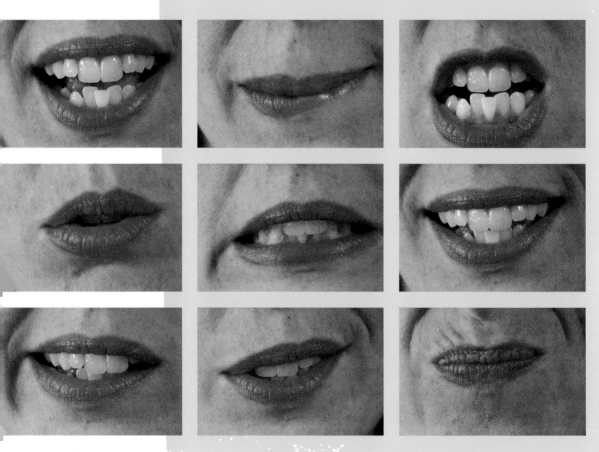

SAY IT AGAIN, SAM

Actors often deliver lines of dialogue over and over, switching their emphasis from one word to another, or changing the tone of their delivery. In this way, they and their director can experiment with the impact of a line or its subtext. You can do the same with written dialogue using italics, word arrangement, and punctuation. For example, consider the following sentences:

"Every goal he sets for *himself*, he achieves."

"Every goal he sets for himself? He achieves it."

"He achieves every goal—every goal—that he sets for himself."

"*Every* goal he sets for himself, he achieves."

Notice how each line reads differently, and implies a different emotional context, even though they're all saying the same thing?

EXERCISE

Write a short scene that includes an important line of dialogue near the beginning. Rewrite the scene, but when you come to the line of dialogue, change the emphasis of the words to convey a slightly different meaning. Continue writing the scene. Did the change in dialogue alter the way you wrote the scene? Try it a third time. Which line "reading" worked best for what you wanted to achieve in the scene? Use the images at left to inspire these various approaches.

THE RHYTHM METHOD

Dialogue is like music. Words, sentences, even paragraphs have a rhythm to them. Change the rhythm and you affect the pace of your story. For example, if you want to convey hurried movement or action, your dialogue might consist of short words, delivered quickly. You could also rely on a few breathless sentences, with no extended moments of silence between them. To slow things down, add thoughtful pauses, punctuation, a more languid delivery or choice of words. Here are some examples:

"No. He just wants the files. I need to get over there so if you know where they are, call my secretary and she'll bring them over. Okay?"

"No… he just wants the files. I need to get over there, sometime. If you know where they are, call my secretary, will you? She can bring them over."

The two sentences are the exact same length, but the feel of them is completely different.

EXERCISE

Consider the photo. Write a scene in which the rhythm of the dialogue reflects the speed at which the characters are moving as well as the topic and tone of their conversation.

THE RIGHT FIT

Do you spend any time thinking about how individual characters speak? One of the challenges of writing dialogue is to make sure each character has a unique voice. They're not all going to speak like you, so a little thought needs to go into recognizing different speech patterns, vocabulary, and colloquialisms. Think about education and cultural backgrounds, occupational and social affiliations. Also, consider what region of the country they're from, or if they're from a foreign country. A lawyer from Alabama is unlikely to speak like a construction worker from Maine.

These differences might be subtle or pronounced. In either case, getting them right takes a good ear and a lot of practice. Too much, and your character will sound like a caricature. Too little, and all your characters will sound like they're speaking with the same voice.

EXERCISE

Ask a friend whose speech patterns and vocabulary are markedly different from your own if you can write down any interesting dialogue she utters during a conversation. Once you've done so, write a scene in which the young woman at left shops for new clothes. Give her the same speech patterns as your friend. When finished, ask your friend to critique the dialogue. Does she recognize it? Does she feel like it's off base or accurate?

CHAPTER FIVE

EMOTIONS

"Acting deals with very delicate emotions. It is not putting up a mask. Each time an actor acts he does not hide; he exposes himself." —JEANNE MOREAU

You're not an actor. I realize that. But if you want your characters to live and breathe, it would behoove you to start thinking like one. Nothing makes characters more real than the verisimilitude of their emotions. Getting there will require some bravery on your part, particularly if you're reticent to portray big emotions in front of your laptop. Get over it—your laptop doesn't care.

There's only one such exercise that asks such effort of you. However, I recommend you make use of it any time you're dealing with strong emotions, particularly big ones. The remaining prompts will help you think about apathy, loneliness, and more.

GOING TO ELEVEN

When describing emotional states, many writers fall back on melo-dramatics or clichés. How can you ensure that the emotions you're writing about ring true?

The following acting exercise may help: Select an emotion. Try acting it out, beginning with its mildest iteration. If you chose fear, you might equate Level 1 with a groaning noise coming from the basement. Imagine how you would feel if there really was such a noise in your home. Try to believe you are experiencing the fear for real. Once you have a handle on the feeling, write down any physical sensations resulting from the exercise. Then, try to imagine Level 2, Level 3, and so on. Believe it. It'll take imagination and a willingness to feel a little foolish, but try as best you can. If you can get to Level 10, you'll either be screaming or curled up in a ball on the ground. In any case, make a note of how you felt at each level, both physically and emotionally. Doing so will enable you to por-tray a more genuine, powerful emotion on the page.

Write a story that explains why the man pictured is so sad. When it comes time to describe how he feels, both physically and emotionally, put yourself through the exercise detailed at left. This time, however, use "unhappiness" as your emotion. Does the exercise help you to better portray his misery?

PARTY OF ONE

Merriam Webster's Collegiate Dictionary, Tenth Edition defines "lonely" as "being without company." It's more complicated than that, of course. Being alone may sometimes make a character's loneliness more pronounced, but their physical distance from others isn't really the problem. It's an issue of emotional isolation. Your protagonist could surround himself with friends and family, even place himself in his lover's arms at night, and still be achingly lonely.

Describing feelings of loneliness (as well as other emotional states) can be treacherous because it's so easy to lapse into cliché. Prior to doing so, the following technique may help give you a new perspective: Find an interesting object and think about the ways in which it might relate to the emotional state of your character. Force yourself to make these connections. The descriptive language you'll generate will enable you to sidestep those worrisome clichés.

EXERCISE

Examine the bench at right. What about it conveys loneliness? When you've compiled a list of ideas, use them to describe your character's emotional state in a story. Perhaps even his physical appearance.

Liar, Liar

Sometimes a character chooses to exhibit an emotional response at odds with what he's really feeling. His reasons for doing so are many and varied, but typically it boils down to manipulation. He wants to avoid a confrontation, disguise an insecurity, inflate his own importance, or acquire something he doesn't really deserve (respect, love, friendship, etc.). If such actions are discovered, others might label him as fake or insincere.

Juxtaposing what a character does with what he really feels can be tricky, particularly if you don't want to come right out and say what he's thinking. Think about body language and any other signals that might convey a character's true emotions.

The woman at right isn't really interested in what her companion is saying. Write a story that illuminates what's happening, how the woman's actions contrast with her emotions, and why. Reveal to the reader her true feelings without explaining what those feelings are.

Who Cares?

We've explored the creation of real emotions, contrasting emotions, and one specific emotion (loneliness). Now, let's consider writing characters who lack any emotion at all. Apathy can be difficult to render effectively on the page. Think about it: How do you describe an apathetic character, someone who doesn't care about her marriage, job, family, friends, life—whatever—without boring your reader?

The first step is to realize that apathy can be just as effective a tool as any emotion. In *Creating Character Emotions*, Ann Hood notes, "the worst misstep is to mistake apathy for boredom ... an apathetic character is not boring. He might be baffling, frustrating, pitiful, or pathological, but never boring."

EXERCISE

Consider the man at the carnival. Write a scene in which his apathy results in humorous consequences. Alternatively, write a scene in which his apathy actually conceals an unspoken desire or need that he is unwilling to express. Refer to p. 100 for ideas on handling contrasting emotional states.

THE SAME, BUT DIFFERENT

Although emotions are universal among all human beings, how they are expressed can be as individual as fingerprints. Think about age, gender, social status, and psychology. Each of these factors influences how your characters exhibit their emotions in different situations.

In the U.S., for example, men are expected to show affection to one another less often, or less overtly, than women. And in some cultures, laughing is impolite. What bearing might this have on a character's sense of humor, or his ability to respond to humor? Remember: Every time you create a new character, be sure to consider all the factors that might have shaped their emotional life. It's a crucial step in developing a character who is both unique and real.

EXERCISE

Create two vastly different characters. Then, write a scene in which the first character must comfort a small child who has lost her stuffed animal. Once you've finished, rewrite the scene but replace the first character with the second. How do their responses differ? Is it clear how experience shapes the expression of one's emotions?

Emotional Wreck

Strong emotions are common in fiction. Your characters experience great stress, intense passion, incredible sadness, and extraordinary joy. When you write such emotional high points, try to make sure that you're not going out of your way to manipulate the feelings of your readers as well. They can sense it when you do, and it has a detrimental effect. You know the sensation. You're watching a perfectly good film and then, because the director loses confidence in the power of his scene, the music swells in an attempt to tell you exactly what you should be feeling. Don't push your reader this way. If you've built the scene properly, and made certain that readers can relate to your characters, they'll feel what you want them to. After all, an author is meant to be invisible. Don't make your presence known with fabricated, overwrought excess.

EXERCISE

Your protagonist and his longtime girl-friend have finally decided to get married. It's a very emotional day for both of them. Write the story of their wedding ceremony. Make it funny, unusual, and real. Give it an extreme emotional highpoint. Then ask yourself, am I letting the quality of the writing do the work, or am I manipulating the reader?

CHAPTER SIX

ENDINGS

> "Whatever the specific events of your story ...
> things can't go on this way much longer.
> Something has to give." —NANCY KRESS

Like everything with a beating heart, your story can only live for so long before reaching its natural end. It's how you choose to finish things that make this chapter so important. Every decision you make informs how the reader will feel about your efforts once the final page is turned. Will you wrap things up, neat as a pin, or do you want your story to resonate long after it's been slipped back on the shelf, huddled amongst its brethren?

Each of these "ending" exercises is designed to help you consider such things, from the denouement to the epilogue, last paragraph to final line. It's your one opportunity to say goodbye and make good on any lingering promises you made to the reader.

COOLING DOWN

Your climax is the dramatic high point of your story. By the time your reader finishes it, she will be excited, satisfied, thoughtful—perhaps even physically and emotionally drained. Now what? Everything that happens between this point and your final line is the denouement. Its purpose, as noted by Nancy Kress in *Beginnings, Middles & Ends*, is to show readers "the consequences of the plot and the fate of any characters not accounted for in the climax."

Another way to think of it is the cool down after a vigorous workout. You stretch, shower, and slow your heart, easing your body back into its regular operating mode. Your denouement operates similarly, easing readers back into reality while providing the emotional satisfaction of closure. Some authors choose to throw one last surprise or two at readers before departing. If you opt to do the same, and the tone of it is markedly different than the balance of your denouement, consider handling such moments in an epilogue (see p. 113).

see p. 113

EXERCISE

After finally having given into their passions against the will of friends and family, two lovers must part forever. Write the denouement that follows the climax. Be sure to address the consequences of their actions as well as the fates of any other major characters.

A CHANGE OF SCENERY

Like prologues, epilogues are used when the tone, location, viewpoint, or time period of the denouement are far removed from that of the climax. In such cases, the details of the denouement will take place in an epilogue instead. It's possible to have both a denouement and an epilogue if you have a lot to say, or have several different viewpoints to represent. In such cases, save the epilogue for those conclusive elements that are most different from your primary storyline.

Strip Tease, by Carl Hiaasen, features an excellent (and funny) example of epilogue. It's clear from the first line that the viewpoint, time, and location have all shifted substantially from that of the climax. And Hiaasen quickly brings readers up to speed on the whereabouts and fates of the remaining characters. If you've never read Hiaasen, I recommend you at least check out this epilogue.

EXERCISE

Your climax focuses upon the final confrontation between a father and his wayward daughter, mid-summer in New York City. Write an epilogue that tells us what happened afterward, noting that the father now finds himself in the environment pictured.

Promises, Promises

When a reader picks up your story, he intuits that certain promises are being made. He expects you to deliver, which is why he bought your book. Fail to do so and your reader will feel his money has been wasted. "But I haven't made any such promise," you protest. Well, yes, you have, even if you weren't aware of it.

In an adventure novel, your reader expects a victorious hero. In romance, a successful love affair. In mystery, a logical, yet challenging, solution. See what I mean? Even if your work doesn't fit neatly into specific genre pigeonholes, you're still promising a resolution in line with any expectations you encouraged (consciously or subconsciously) in chapter one. For example, if your heroine is driven to the edge of suicide by the loss of her one true love and the family farm, she better get them back, or in some way come to terms with the situation. If you fail to deliver, your readers will be confused and disappointed.

EXERCISE

Write a short story in which your protagonist's boyfriend gives her an ultimatum: Give up smoking or we're through. Write about her approach to dealing with the situation. Keep in mind that she doesn't have to give up smoking in order to fulfill the promise you make to the reader.

Cliffhangers

Cliffhangers are those denouements left open-ended, indicating that some aspect of the story will remain unresolved until the next book or film. The most effective cliffhangers have an emotional impact on your protagonist, as well as physical. Consider, for example, *The Empire Strikes Back*. After the climax, Luke and Leia survive to fight another day. Yet their friends remain in grave danger and Luke must confront some crippling personal issues. Viewers can't wait to see how the physical and emotional conflicts are resolved.

EXERCISE

Write another denouement, following a climactic confrontation between your hero and her antagonist. This time, however, don't end things so neat and tidy. In the last few paragraphs, your hero finds a key. What is the significance of this key, and how might it lead to your hero's next adventure? Be sure that finding the key engages your hero emotionally as well as intellectually.

THIS WAY OUT

By the time you reach the climax of your story, a great deal of tension will have been built. The reader wants a satisfying payoff. So how do you resolve the climax? You have options, of course; different ways in which the story might end. How do you determine which one to use? After all, Romeo and Juliet didn't really have to die. Did they?

Your climax must be:

Emotionally satisfying. You owe it to the reader to meet their expectations. These expectations could be required by a specific genre, or by any promises you made earlier in the story. Also, be sure to resolve any dangling plot threads.

Exciting. This doesn't mean action packed necessarily, only that the scene should be one of the story's most intense and absorbing.

Logical. This doesn't mean there can't be a twist or surprise ending, only that the ending you choose makes sense, given all that has come before it.

Your protagonist has been trying to avoid the local gangs roaming his neighborhood. He's been told it's in his best interest to join. After weeks of evading them successfully, he's cornered in the alley pictured. He makes for the door beneath the arrow, but it's locked. Write what happens next, keeping in mind the criteria noted above.

The Final Word

Your last line is nearly as important as your first. It is the final thought your reader takes away from the story. What should it be? Do you want the story to be 100 percent conclusive, so that your reader can turn out the light and look forward to their next literary excursion? Or do you want it to resonate for a time, keeping him involved long after the final page has been turned? Perhaps it establishes the next step for your characters, saying to the reader, in essence: "Our time together is through, but the people you've come to care about aren't done living. And there may be more to come."

Look back over the endings you've written so far, pick one and focus on the last line. Ask yourself if the line sends the message you intended. What is that message? If it's not clear, then you may need to revise it.

EXERCISE

Write the denouement of a story about a woman whose home was destroyed in a summer storm. She's leaving town, hoping to find a brighter future elsewhere. The last line ends the story at the setting pictured. What's your final message for the reader?

122

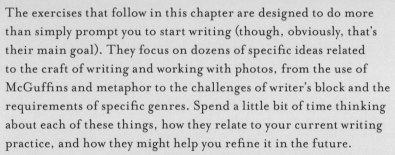

CHAPTER SEVEN

STORY STARTERS

"Ideas are like rabbits. You get a couple and learn how to handle them, and pretty soon you have a dozen." —**JOHN STEINBECK**

The exercises that follow in this chapter are designed to do more than simply prompt you to start writing (though, obviously, that's their main goal). They focus on dozens of specific ideas related to the craft of writing and working with photos, from the use of McGuffins and metaphor to the challenges of writer's block and the requirements of specific genres. Spend a little bit of time thinking about each of these things, how they relate to your current writing practice, and how they might help you refine it in the future.

Try to write at least two full pages for each exercise. This may seem daunting, but the benefits you'll reap will make it well worth the effort.

{123}

❧ Solve the Puzzle ❧

One of the easiest ways to get your brain fired up for writing is to present it with a question that needs to be answered, or a puzzle that has to be solved. This makes the act of writing more of a game than a chore. The perception of writing as hard work is what keeps many of us from actually accomplishing anything, so let's change that mindset from the outset.

What's nice about images is that they not only indicate what the puzzle might be, but often provide clues for crafting the solution. Look for tiny details in the background as well as the foreground. Think about the apparent time of day, location, and weather. Mine the image for whatever information you can. In some cases, it will be minimal. That's okay. It'll force you to be that much more imaginative.

EXERCISE

Examine the image at right. The obvious questions are: What happened here? Why is this bike on the ground? What circumstances would account for its abandonment? Make up whatever explanation most interests you and see how much material it generates. Solve the puzzle.

Time for Suspense

Alfred Hitchcock used a straightforward technique to ratchet up the tension in his films. First, he made it clear that something dangerous or frightening was going to occur at a specific time to a specific character. Then he made the audience wait … and wait … and wait until it happened. Sounds simple to do, but there's a fine line between building suspense and boring your audience. Lesser filmmakers (and writers) prove with depressing regularity how tricky it is. Building suspense is impossible if your audience doesn't care about your endangered character and nothing of interest happens during your build up to the moment of climax. Don't forget about the basics on your way to the payoff.

EXERCISE

Try your hand at creating a scenario like the one described above and see if you can make the payoff worth the wait. Refer to the photo at left to establish your setting, and use the clock tower to determine the time frame in which the events will take place.

Some writers will admit that they don't really think too much about the specifics of their story prior to writing it; neither its basic theme nor how it will play out. Many don't even bother envisioning an ending. The story simply comes into existence as the protagonist lives through it. In this way, the writer acts as much chronicler as creator.

I have found that this technique—depending on your characters to show you the way—is a good method for coming up with story ideas as well. Think of a character you've written before, one you feel comfortable writing about without any set goal or storyline in mind. If you deposited this character in a random situation, do you know how he would act? If so, your knowledge of the character's personality and desires will drive his involvement in the scene to its logical conclusion.

EXERCISE

Examine the image at left. Observe the expression on the face of the man and imagine the cause of his amusement. Then, replace him with your favorite character and write a story about the incident and the role your character plays in its resolution.

Everyday

The most frightening moments in fiction are often those grounded in everyday life. In Stephen King's *Pet Sematary*, for example, one of the most memorable, chilling passages has nothing to do with zombie cats or Indian graveyards (which, according to the sales copy, were what made the book so terrifying). It was the scene when Gage, the protagonist's young son, wandered away from home.

The incident that followed resonates with far more power than anything else in the book. And yet, there wasn't anything supernatural—or even malicious—about the incident. Another good example from King: The electrocution of prisoner Edward Delacroix in *The Green Mile*. No ghosts or vampires in sight, but all the more gut wrenching because of it.

Horrors

Swimming the Stream of Consciousness

Big inspiration can come from a very small source. Think of the most insignificant thing you can, say the tail of a dog. Ask yourself, what is the dog's tail doing and what does that signify? Is it wagging, tucked between its legs, or pointing straight back? Where is the dog? Is this location causing the dog anxiety, happiness, or fear (any one of which would be reflected in the action of its tail)? Who owns the dog and what are they doing?

By imaging the details surrounding this "insignificant" detail, you create a setting, a situation, and a character that has to deal with the situation. That's your story. Doing this exercise helps keep your imagination percolating and enables you to find ideas in the smallest of details.

EXERCISE

The cactus needle at left is your starting point. Imagine the setting surrounding the cactus. What are the difficulties and pleasures of this type of environment? Ask yourself who might be there and why. How does the setting affect the characters you've imagined? Does it also help inform your plot? Write the scene.

The Coming Storm

Anticipation is one thing (see the "suspense" exercise on p. 127), but dread is something altogether different. And a fate that simply cannot be avoided, overcome, or bargained with inspires the worst kind of dread. Putting your character into this type of situation allows you to explore extreme mental and emotional states that more commonplace events don't allow for.

Consider, for example, the film *Titanic*, by director James Cameron. You know the ending before the movie starts, at least so far as the ship is concerned. Everything that happens on screen is overshadowed by the fact that these characters, so happy and in love, are going to be put through trials unlike anything they could have possibly imagined. A sense of dread clings to every emotion, high and low, throughout the film, providing power to the simplest scenes.

EXERCISE

Create a story in which a character is faced with an unavoidable fate. Use the image at left as your inspiration and write at least 1,000 words detailing how he deals with this "coming storm."

Escape

What follows is a problem-solving exercise that will test your ingenuity and writing ability. You're going to put a character into a difficult, potentially life-threatening situation for which there is no obvious solution and write about her efforts to escape until she does.

Although the specifics of this challenge are described in the exercise below, don't read ahead. In order for this to be a proper trial, you need to develop your character prior to knowing what the situation is. Pay particular attention to her physical condition, personality, and background. If you think you're up to it, try relating the situation in which she finds herself to an internal conflict that must also be resolved.

EXERCISE

Your character is enjoying an early morning hike when the ground opens up beneath her feet. She falls into a previously unknown cave. Write about her efforts to escape until she succeeds. The next time you are faced with frustration, writer's block, or worse, remind yourself to be as resolute as your character. Solving the problem is never simply a matter of method. But it's always a matter of will.

Missing Pieces

When you're in need of inspiration, you can't do much better than look at a partial image—something in which the subject is only half seen, and where the important action is taking place just out of sight. Like an optical illusion, our brains automatically move to fill in the missing pieces, forcing us to draw our own conclusions about what's really going on.

Write a story based on the image at left. Examine the picture closely for clues as to what might be happening. If you can't find any, make some up! Good storytellers can't stop themselves from completing the picture.

❧ WANT vs. NEED ❧

Powerful writing often results when you submit your character to a difficult internal conflict. One such conflict is the opposition of what they want versus what they need. Exploring these two ideas tells the reader a great deal about what motivates your character. In the case of your protagonist, it also provides an engine for your story. Why is your character doing what he's doing? What does he want? What does he need? Are they related?

Another thought: How does the difference between want and need change the nature of your character's motivation? Which is the greater motivator of the two? The potential loss of either provides a great basis for conflict and dramatic storytelling, but when a character is forced to give up one for the other, the drama can be almost unbearable.

EXERCISE

Using the image at right, write a scene in which a character sees something through the window that they want more than anything else in the world. Getting it will mean giving up something they need. Then, write a scene in which the situation is reversed. Both have power. Which one works best for you?

ᛥ Meet Cute ᛥ

If you've been to the movies, you've seen this bit a hundred times. You know what I'm talking about—the scene in which our protagonist and her romantic opposite number run into one another for the first time. The meeting is meant to be humorous and endearing, but it's almost always contrived and rather dull. Sometimes a film can pull it off. (Think *When Harry Met Sally*.) At other times, it simply doesn't work. (Consider *How to Lose a Guy in 10 Days*.) This scene, and its execution, has become so commonplace it has gained entry into the filmmaking lexicon as the "meet cute." No matter what the circumstances, it's your job to make that first important meeting unique and engaging.

EXERCISE

Imagine your romantically inclined duo at an outdoor market, shopping for their week's worth of groceries. Write a scene in which they meet for the first time while reaching for the same box of berries. There is no avoiding this cliché. Do whatever you can to turn it into a real moment between real people.

NAUGHTY VOYEUR

Choosing the point of view (POV) in which to write your story can be a tricky thing. Almost every author goes through that dreaded moment in which they realize, halfway through a three-hundred-page novel (or a fifteen-page short story for that matter) that the piece would work better if told from first person point of view rather than third person. Been there. Done that. Hated it.

But experimenting with POV can be fun. Use the following exercise to get a different perspective on who your protagonist is and how others might perceive him.

Rather than writing about your protagonist using a standard POV, examine his actions as if you were a documentary filmmaker. You are a subjective observer writing a nonfiction piece about a living, breathing person. He will not notice you, nor will your presence influence his actions. Start your observations at the beach, where he patiently waits. As you write, think about his movements, body language, and nervous habits—things that you might not have considered were you not observing him in this fashion. Can you use these tiny details to make him a richer character?

EMBRACE THE CLICHÉ

On p. 143, we attempted to take a specific cliché and enliven it. Can you think, however, of a situation when using a cliché actually helps a story by meeting reader expectations rather than exceeding them? Is there value to providing your audience with something they've seen before, even many times over?

Think Columbo, James Bond, or any one of a hundred romance novels. To one degree or another, the audiences for these literary and cinematic adventures know exactly what their favorite clichés are and fully expect them to appear on schedule. The heroine will overcome adversity to be loved by her rugged, yet surprisingly tender, man; just as he begins to exit the room, Columbo will stop, turn around and say, "Just one more question, if you don't mind;" and Bond will crack wise while using his latest Q-device to vanquish the villain's thuggish henchman.

EXERCISE

The image at left shows what is oftentimes a cliché moment in storytelling. In this exercise, play up the cliché for all it's worth, keeping in mind what part of it your audience most wants to experience. Providing readers with something they've seen before can be effective if you do it with skill and style.

Characters in Motion

Writers often allow their narrative to get swept up in the kind of action that leaves their characters behind. When this happens, it's because the characters have become secondary to the spectacle. Spectacle, no matter how dazzling, is empty and meaningless if it doesn't advance your story or provide your characters with an opportunity to reveal more of themselves to the reader.

Some writers, like Lee Child (*Without Fail*) and Wilbur Smith (*River God*), manage to subject their characters to all manner of abuse, while at the same time using the chaos to help further define them, or move the plot forward. Others … well, let's just say that it's tougher than it looks.

Think about the chaos of an amusement park. Write 1,000 words that effectively capture the sensory overload on display. At the same time, use the various park elements to advance your scene without taking the focus from your characters and the story that needs to be told. Don't let your story be overwhelmed by motion, flash, and dazzle.

WRITE WHAT YOU (DON'T) KNOW

Many books on writing tell you to write what you know. I say bull. Don't be afraid to write about something you know little about. If it motivates you to write a story, then do it. Your job, first and foremost, is to write about interesting characters dealing with interesting problems. The grunt work of research and rewriting can come later. The important thing is to ride the wave of inspiration for as long as it lasts; get the story out of your head and onto the page.

In his book, *On Writing*, Stephen King says much the same thing: "When you step away from the 'write what you know' rule, research becomes inevitable, and it can add a lot to your story. Just don't end up with the tail wagging the dog; remember that you are writing a novel, not a research paper. The story always comes first."

EXERCISE

Your character is a construction worker whose job is to operate the machine pictured. He's exhausted from working overtime, but continues to do so in order to provide for his family. Write a scene in which this fatigue affects his performance, possibly in a dangerous way.

For the Love of the Genre

All too often, beginning writers feel self-conscious about writing genre fiction, even if their love of the genre is what made them want to be a writer in the first place. These writers are under the assumption that "legitimate" writing has to be literary in nature, as far removed from the "ghettos" of science fiction, horror, fantasy, and romance as possible. I'm not sure how these assumptions began, or why they persist, but it's clear that somewhere along the way genre fiction got a bad rap. Certainly it can be just as literary as any other type of fiction.

If you suffer from a similar inferiority complex, get over it. Trying to write fiction that you're not passionate about will only lead to failure. You'll either get bored or write badly. Embrace the genre you love. It's your passion that makes the act of writing worth the effort.

THE STRANGER EFFECT

Good story ideas often appear like a stranger on your doorstep: unexpected, a little mysterious, and usually wanting something. In this case, your story wants to be told. That's why it came to you. You're the writer, yes?

Keeping this description in mind, think about how such qualities affect the people with whom the stranger interacts. The potential for drama is rich, even in the most innocent of situations.

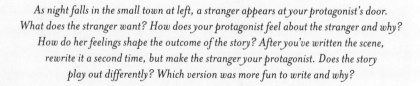

As night falls in the small town at left, a stranger appears at your protagonist's door. What does the stranger want? How does your protagonist feel about the stranger and why? How do her feelings shape the outcome of the story? After you've written the scene, rewrite it a second time, but make the stranger your protagonist. Does the story play out differently? Which version was more fun to write and why?

Setting the Mood

Setting is not simply the time and place in which your story happens. It's also a tool used to convey mood, tone, character, and more subtle elements of storytelling, such as tension and foreshadowing.

Let's examine mood specifically. Setting can be used to 1) reflect the mood of a character or situation, 2) act as counterpoint to the mood of a character or situation, and 3) foreshadow a change in mood. In the first case, your character's glum outlook might be mirrored by the gray forest through which she walks. In the second, her high spirits might stand in stark contrast to that same setting, implying that her joy is so great as to be unaffected by the surrounding gloom. In the final case, she may be happy in a setting that reflects her mood—but gathering clouds indicate that this happy moment isn't going to last.

EXERCISE

Focus on establishing a palpable mood, one that reflects the mindset of your protagonist. Get started by using the image at left. Then, slowly change the setting so that her mood stands out against it. Does the transition help illustrate the effect noted above?

Grand Designs

The term "set piece" denotes a virtuosic scene in a story. Something designed by its creator specifically to impress his audience. Even if you've never heard the term before, you've seen it played out many times. Think of the aria from Aida, a Harry Potter Quidditch match, or the heist scene from *Rififi*. Some stories are built almost entirely around set pieces. Dan Brown's *Angels & Demons* is a good example.

The problem is, set pieces can become so grand and so focused on delivering excitement that readers lose interest and get bored—right when the author expects them to be amazed. At these moments, the set piece has taken our focus away from the characters, and inadvertently made the story about itself.

EXERCISE

Set pieces can be a great help when you're trying to come up with a story idea. In this exercise, come up with an interesting set piece first, based on the image at left. Envision the story that would lead your characters to the set piece, then write it.

NEVER SAY DULL

There are some authors who defy all the rules of fiction by making the seemingly very dull absolutely fascinating. These writers have such a gift for dialogue, note-perfect characterization, and vivid description, that they can write about the act of slicing cheese and make it just as compelling as a courtroom rebuttal or guns-a-blazing action scene.

Take Ian Fleming, for example, an author who is no longer given the time of day beyond an obligatory nod at the beginning of each new James Bond film. In *Casino Royale* (the book), Fleming writes a scene in which Bond spends four pages explaining to another character (and, conveniently, the reader) the game of baccarat. Soon after, Fleming devotes twenty more pages to an actual baccarat game. And it doesn't get boring for a minute.

EXERCISE

Write like Fleming. Using the image at left as your inspiration, write a story in which seemingly little occurs, but every action, no matter how small, is of great importance to the characters involved.

Girl,

There's an old writing adage that says once a story starts to slow down, have someone burst through the door unexpectedly. This technique may have worked back in the days of pulp fiction and classic comics, when action came first, logic second. But today?

Regardless, it doesn't mean that a well-planned surprise can't work wonders for your fiction, and give you a boost of inspiration as well, particularly if you're suffering from writer's block. Whatever the motive behind your surprise, make sure that it 1) ties back into the main plot, 2) reveals something important about your character, and 3) comes across as believable, rather than contrived.

Interrupted.

Write a story in which your protagonist sits in a diner eating a piece of cake. She and her friends are trying to resolve a personal issue of great importance without success. Have an unexpected interruption provide your protagonist with the means to resolve the problem.

You Are What You Eat

The quality of what you read informs the quality of what you write. In other words, if you read great fiction, you're more likely to write great fiction. The opposite also holds true.

Consider: For decades, American comic books were thought to be strictly for kids (there were, of course, exceptions). Although the audience was actually much broader than that, the stories and dialogue were often juvenile and, in many cases, poorly written. It seemed as if most comic book writers had learned their craft from, well, reading comic books. Then, in the early 1980s, things began to change. A new breed of writers (including Alan Moore, Neil Gaiman, Matt Wagner, Dave Sim, and others) with more literary aspirations (and backgrounds) helped transform what was a stagnant medium into one of unlimited potential.

No matter what your genre of choice, make sure to read the best possible writers working in it. Doing so *will* influence the quality of what you write.

EXERCISE

Write a story about a superhero—but write it as well and as realistically as you can. Any topic will be taken seriously if it's well written. Aspire to this, no matter if you're writing a jungle adventure or a gothic romance.

Recess and Renewal

When you're suffering from writer's block, it may be due to apathy, fatigue, or familiarity. It's possible that you need to step away from your current story and try something new. This new tale doesn't have to be long or complex—only enough to re-engage your imagination and take your mind off of the larger task at hand. Consider it a recess of sorts.

My favorite exercise of this type is to throw a character into the deep end of a situation or environment that they know nothing about. It's fun, the drama is immediate, and the opportunities to describe unusual people, smells, sights, and sounds are unlimited.

EXERCISE

Try this little writing vacation on for size and see if you don't come back renewed and refreshed. Craft a short piece about someone nearing the end of a long journey. They're about to disembark from the ship that has been their home for several weeks. The port before them is foreign; its people and customs unlike anything they've experienced before.

Devil's Advocate

One of the most difficult things to pull off when writing a character you can't sympathize with is sincerity. If you don't believe, there will be moments when your character doesn't ring true. It's good practice—and often an eye-opening experience—to play devil's advocate.

When preparing to write a character with whom you can't possibly agree, take it upon yourself to argue their case. Be open-minded. Allow the opposing viewpoint its due and do everything you can to substantiate their argument, even if it makes you uncomfortable to do so. Having these insights into how and why characters believe what they do will give your story an added layer of complexity, depth, and believability.

EXERCISE

The images above suggest two characters with differing political philosophies. Determine which point of view you least agree with. This is your protagonist. Write a scene in which he and his antagonist clash over their differing viewpoints. The character you have chosen (the one you disagree with) should win the argument. Make his case irrefutable.

The Vacuum

Have you ever been in a conversation where the person you are speaking to suddenly stops talking? They look at you and wait, expectantly. Usually, you start talking again right away. The need to fill that void of silence can be almost unbearable. Try it the next time you want to negotiate the price of a car, return something at the grocery, or get a better hotel room. Sales people will stumble all over themselves trying to fill up the silence, even if it means capitulating to your request. It's a natural response.

Try to re-create this uncomfortable situation in your writing. It's amazing what will come out of your character's mouth when she's faced with the possibility of conversational "dead air," particularly if she's in the middle of a confession or apology. She'll reveal more than she meant to or start lying.

EXERCISE

Your protagonist is hosting a small happy hour for some new friends. At some point, their corner of the room grows quiet, making it clear that they don't have much to say to one another. How does your character fill the silence? What about her personality dictates the nature of her efforts?

Setting as Story

Sometimes all the inspiration you need for a story is a good setting with a few unusual elements. Take any fashion magazine, for example. In it, you'll find images of bedrooms, boardrooms, apartments, exotic locales, and swanky nightclubs. Set decorators are charged with putting all manner of oddities in the background, in order to make the scene more "real." Most readers never give this level of minutia a second thought, but once you do, you'll discover an endless parade of story ideas every time you stop at the newsstand.

Think about the setting at right, and the kind of story that might take place within it. Look in the background for any interesting details that might help define the specifics of what's happening and why. How do these details bear upon your plot? Write the story and find out.

Related

Need a creative jolt? Your brain likes nothing more than to make connections between seemingly unrelated things. That's why conspiracy theories and mystery novels are so popular. We're obsessed with proving that each unique element in the universe is related to every other element. Physicists call it The Unified Field Theory (UFT)—the belief that all physical phenomena can be explained in terms of a single theoretical framework.

Allow your brain the chance to ponder upon this idea for a bit. From the UFT to biblical creation, human beings have fashioned an endless number of theories about the nature of the universe, our relationship to it, and to one another. Let's test the idea, shall we?

EXERCISE

At left are a number of random items, unrelated in any way. Your job is to come up with a story in which three of these items actually are related, and that relationship plays a major role in the story's outcome.

Misperceptions

What a character *doesn't* know can provide you with great material for story ideas, whether comedy or drama. Consider the hysterical misunderstandings of *Some Like It Hot*, the sinister case of mistaken identity in *North by Northwest*, or the unexpected deceptions of *The Flanders Panel*.

Using this device to generate a story idea is simple. First, assume that whatever it is your character doesn't know is important to his survival or success. Then ask yourself the following four questions:

1) What doesn't your character know?
2) What will happen if he does not find out?
3) What clues inform your character that he's missing crucial information?
4) What does he do to solve the problem?

EXERCISE

Write a story in which everything a character understands about a situation is wrong, using the criteria noted at right and the image at left as your inspiration.

CHALLENGES

Many years ago, I wrote a story about an elderly couple coming to terms with the wife's Alzheimer's disease. It was submitted to a group of my peers for review, at which point I was immediately called on the carpet for being "emotionally dishonest" and "convenient" in my treatment of the disease. They were right, of course. I'd written about what I thought Alzheimer's was like, rather than the reality of it. Serious research was needed—but even that didn't solve the problem.

Writing characters whose physical or mental limitations affect every decision they make can be difficult. Too often, writers fall back upon the limitation as a storytelling tool. Never lose sight of the fact that the character always comes first. Author Mark Haddon maintains this focus admirably in *The Curious Incident of the Dog in the Night-Time*, an exceptional novel featuring an autistic protagonist.

EXERCISE

Write a scene in which your paraplegic protagonist must accomplish one of life's daily tasks, like bathing or cooking dinner. As you do so, make sure that the character continues to drive the action, rather than letting the disability become the focus of the story.

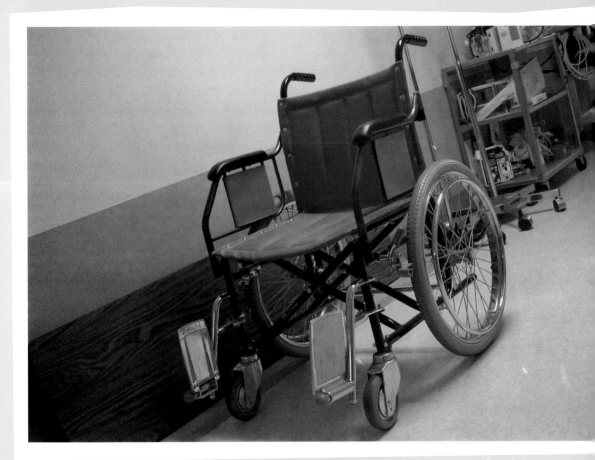

The McGuffin

One of Alfred Hitchcock's well-known methods for developing a story was to come up with a person, an object, information, or a place of great importance to the various characters in the piece. It is this subject—the "McGuffin"—that fuels their various motivations.

Developing a McGuffin of your own is an easy way to come up with story ideas. The item must represent something that at least two different parties are interested in possessing. It could be an object, knowledge, or status. Exactly *what* your McGuffin is really isn't that important. Who possesses it currently (if anyone) and what characters are willing to do to get it—that's the focus of your story.

EXERCISE

Referring to the image at right, craft a story in which this seemingly everyday item represents something of great importance to your protagonist. She wants to possess it, but so does someone else. Write about the conflict this causes.

VISCERAL RESPONSES

There's something particularly entertaining about writing horror stories. Indulging in nightmare imagery and examining the darker side of human nature are only some of the attractions. There's a sense of giddy fun associated with such subject matter, when realized as fiction. Perhaps it's the cathartic sensation of "living" through our worst fears, or maybe we're simply more ghoulish than we like to believe. Whatever the reason, ideas and images that lend themselves to feelings of fear and terror make for great storytelling opportunities.

EXERCISE

While investigating a seemingly abandoned building, your protagonist stumbles across a dead body lying askew in the grimy bathtub pictured. Upon closer examination, she notices something particularly bone-chilling. Write the details of this scene along with what happens next. Do whatever you can to give yourself the shivers.

THE BETTER STORY

As writers, we tend to fall in love with specific story ideas—the ones that hit us in a flash, providing all sorts of energy, excitement, and inspiration. And in the beginning, when everything is shiny and new, those ideas often seem brilliant. Sometimes they are.

Be willing, however, to regularly and objectively evaluate how good your protagonist's story really is. Is it as absorbing and interesting as you'd hoped? If not, think about your secondary characters. Do any of their stories seem more interesting? Be willing to recognize the fact that there may be another character whose tale is more worthy of being told.

EXERCISE

Examine the photo at left. You might assume that your protagonist is the man about to be hit by a car. Write about the incident from his perspective. Then, write the same scene, but from the point of view of the driver. Which version most intrigues you? Which version is most effective?

KEEPING IT REAL

The most critical element of your story is emotional truth. What I mean by that is, no matter what else is happening, no matter what strange, unlikely, or downright impossible events are taking place, there needs to be a kernel of truth with which your reader can identify. When this level of realism takes a backseat to plot and spectacle, the reader stops identifying with the protagonist and begins to lose interest. Even in the most outlandish of tales, say, for example, *The Fellowship of the Ring* by J.R.R. Tolkien, the reader remains invested because the emotions are real. Frodo is astonished, frustrated, and frightened—sometimes all at once. He longs to return home, but can't. He faces loneliness, despair, and even death. We empathize because we can relate.

EXERCISE

Write a story in which your character discovers an absurd, unlikely, or fantastic item in the box pictured. Make sure that, no matter how bizarre things get, your character's emotions and actions ring true.

3

...ing and can f...

...and all knowledge, ...

...cy that can ...

...have not love, I am ...

...e all I possess to the poor, ...

...nder my body to the flames,[?] ...

...ve not love, I gain nothing.

[4]Love is patient,[f] love is kind...

...oes not envy,[u] it does not boast, ...

...ot proud.[u] [5]It is not rude, it ...

...self-seeking,[v] it is not easily a...

...it keeps no record of wrong...

...es not delight in evilly ...

...he truth.[z] [7]It always ...

...h, always hop...

Word by**Word**

No matter how long the journey, it always begins with a first step. Until you take it, you haven't *really* committed to a direction or destination. It's the same with writing. You can think, plan, out-line, storyboard, and doodle all you want. But until you actually begin, it's all just a lot of dreamy intentions.

Start with a single word if you must. Pick one that suggests an interesting idea, setting, or character. Think about the sentence you want supporting that word. Write it down. Think about what a wonderful paragraph you could build around that sentence. Do it. Then write a page worthy of that paragraph, and a chapter worthy of that page. One step at a time can be slow going. But one step at a time is how you get to where you want to be.

Choose one word from those shown in the photograph at left. Make sure you like the word—that the sound and shape of it intrigues you. Write a sentence including the word, then a paragraph to support the sentence. Continue until you've written at least 1,000 words.

Have you ever experienced a smell, a sound, or a piece of music that triggered a particularly vivid memory? The memory is often so strong it feels as if you're reliving it. When fiction achieves this level of reality—the sense of experiencing a specific time or place without actually being there—it becomes almost hypnotic. As a writer, your goal is to imbue every piece you write with this same extraordinary quality. But how do you achieve it? Actors rely on sense memories (recalled through sensory impressions of an event) to help re-create the reality of firsthand experience. Tapping into such memories helps them to cry on cue, fly into a rage, or "believe" that they are in love. Try it for yourself and see if it doesn't help you create a more believable, engrossing story.

EXERCISE

Think about the last time you listened to someone play a violin. Remember the setting, sounds, and mood. How did these elements make you feel? Write a scene in which your protagonist tells a friend or lover about a secret that will change their lives. Set the scene in the rich background you just re-created.

THE MUSIC OF
MEMORY

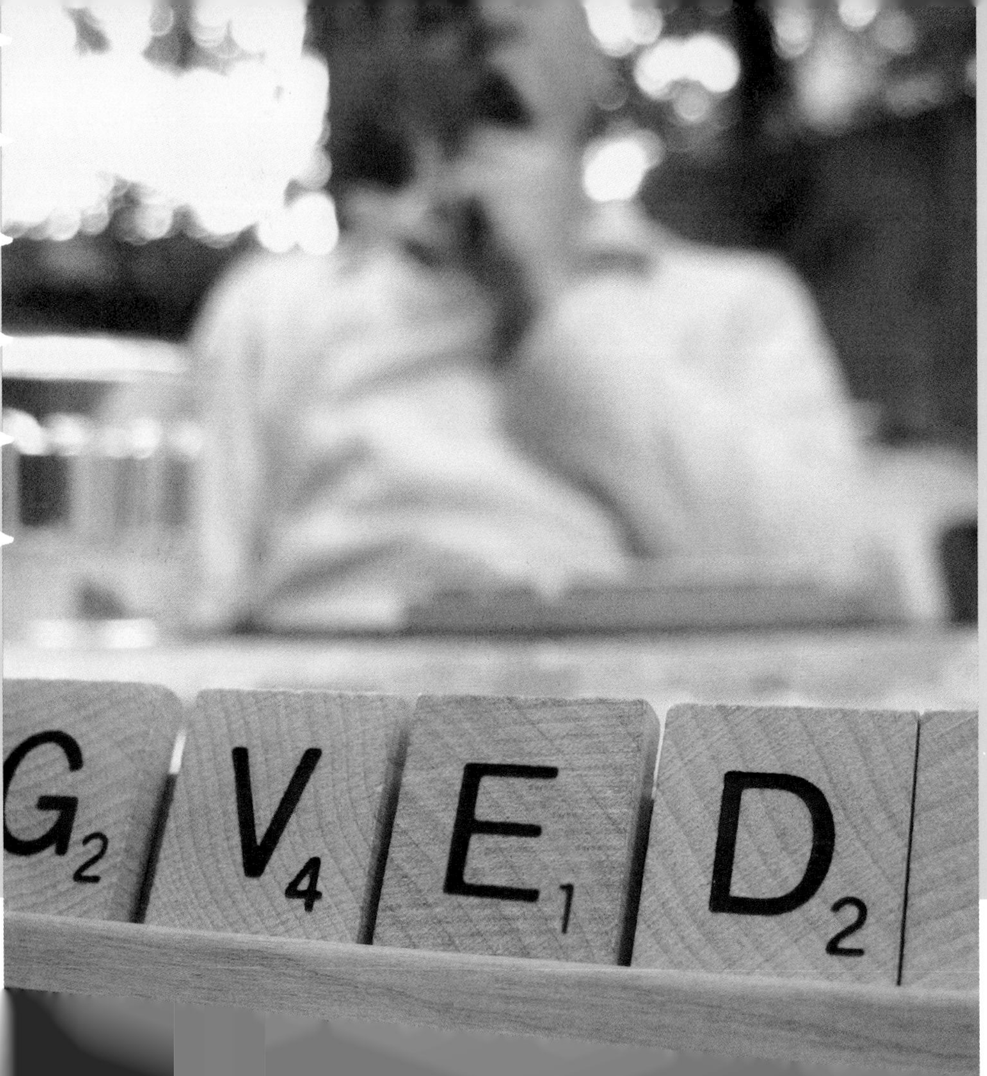
G2 V4 E1 D2

Everywhere an Opportunity

If you're having trouble coming up with ideas, the best advice you'll ever get is to ask "what if?" Most texts devoted to writing fiction will tell you this. And though it may sound trite (particularly if this is the 47th time you've heard it), there's no denying that it works.

No matter how often you use it, the "what if?" question never loses its power. Pairing it with an image can make it even more effective. Photos, even randomly chosen ones, provide you with a subject to think about, and possibly a setting or context that will spur you to pose your own "what if?" Give it a try.

EXERCISE

My "what if?" question for the photo at left was, "What if one of the people playing Scrabble began to spell out the following words: being – watched – family – in – danger – please – help?" Come up with your own "what if?" question based on the photo, then write the story.

Raise the Stakes

In his excellent book *Writing the Breakout Novel*, Donald Maass advises writers to "raise the stakes" in their stories. Why is this idea important? Because the greater the stakes, the more your reader will care about what's happening and how it turns out.

For example: A stranger levels a gun at your protagonist, Rick, just as he's leaving the office. The man forces Rick to drive to the desert. Once there, he shoots Rick, steals his briefcase, and drives away. Our hero, however, is tough. He struggles to his feet, knowing that he must somehow warn his superiors about the theft before bleeding to death. The briefcase contained information critical to national security. Pretty high stakes, wouldn't you agree? But what if, prior to driving away, the stranger receives a call on his cell phone and is instructed to eliminate Rick's family? Rick also discovers that the stranger intends to use the information to help a terrorist assassinate the President. Now we have a story!

EXERCISE

Write a story in which a wife loses her husband in the setting pictured. She must find him in order to relieve the babysitter back home. Once you're into the story, raise the stakes. There's something else happening that makes relieving the babysitter the least of her worries.

BETWEEN HERE AND THERE

It's not hard to get ideas. But some days, it's hard to know what to do with them. Where are you going? What is your ending? How will you get there?

Some authors determine their story's final scene well before they start writing. Doing so, they believe, gives them something specific to work towards and eliminates the possibility of a meandering storyline. If you're having a hard time getting to the end of a story, maybe you have the same need. Try the following exercise and see if it helps:

Imagine an intriguing ending before worrying about anything else. Make it a really cool one. Then think about what it would take for your character to end up there. What challenges might she have to overcome along the way, and, of course, what incident thrusts her into the story in the first place? This method of working backward can help you figure out the plot points you couldn't see looking forward.

Your story begins with "She tore open the envelope, her hands shaking."
The photo above is where it ends. Write your way there.

Your Personal Trainer

You've heard the analogy before. Your writing ability is like a muscle. If you want to strengthen it, or keep it in shape, you need to write regularly and often. But more than that, you need to write with care. Anyone with a thermos of coffee and a weekend of free time can crank out ten pages of material. It's the quality of the writing that counts.

A personal trainer will tell you when your form is off, encourage you to increase your reps, or add weight to the barbell. Unfortunately, writers don't often get personal trainers. They can, however, get something even better: an objective reader. This is a friend or acquaintance you can trust to tell you exactly what's good—and bad—about your work. Someone whose opinion you value, but also someone who is encouraging and constructive in his criticism.

EXERCISE

Three days ago, a young boy drowned in the lake pictured. His father, aimlessly walking along the shore, spots something that changes what he believes about his son's death. Write this scene. When finished, hand it over to your objective reader. Be open to their feedback. Can any of their suggestions improve your work?

The Magic of Metaphors

In "The Behavior of Hawkweeds," from Andrea Barrett's award-winning short story collection *Ship Fever*, the author reveals the feelings and motivations behind the actions of her protagonist, Antonia, by making metaphors out of plants and hybridization experiments. It may sound odd, but it works spectacularly well. Doing so enables Barrett to craft a compelling story that's not only filled with lovely descriptions and precise language, but also richly layered with meaning throughout.

That's one of the gifts of metaphor: it enables the writer to explore complex, abstract, or even taboo topics without slowing down to explain everything through heavy-handed dialogue or narrative exposition. From *Star Trek* to Shakespeare, a masterfully constructed metaphor can add depth, significance, and resonance to the simplest of scenes.

EXERCISE

Your protagonist and his friend are drifting apart. They don't seem to be able to discuss the reasons why. Write about their final uncomfortable conversation, which takes place at a coffee shop. Use the coffee cup as a metaphor for what's really going on, and how your protagonist feels about it.

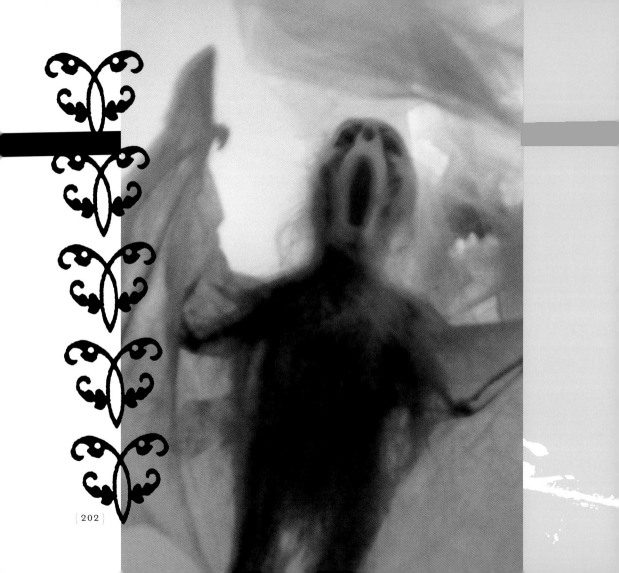

The Buffy Effect

Emotional truth in storytelling is critical to writing a story that resonates with readers. It's particularly important when working in such genres as science fiction, fantasy, or horror. All too often, real human emotion is made secondary to the spectacle of setting and plot.

Consider this scene: The lone young woman goes down into the dark basement. The lights don't work. She hears heavy breathing. Does she run for help? No, strangely enough. And that's when the audience starts to lose interest. When characters stop acting like real people with real feelings, there's no reason to keep watching—or reading.

When you write such tales, consider Joss Whedon. Whatever you think of his television creations (including *Buffy the Vampire Slayer*), his personal rule has always been that every story must be grounded in real emotions, even if monsters are the ones experiencing them. The coffins, spells, and spaceships? Props, really, and nothing more.

EXERCISE

Write a story in which your protagonist encounters the apparition at left. Make this incident as creepy, terrifying, and outrageous as you like, but keep the emotions of your character grounded in reality.

{ 203 }

MULTIPLE EXPOSURES

If you really want to get a better understanding of how your characters will react in different situations, try writing a scene in which multiple characters are present when something important happens. Write the scene multiple times, from the viewpoint of a different character each time.

Provide them with the same general information, but take careful note of how they interpret and react to it differently. This can tell you more about the character than you thought you knew, in addition to providing you with an idea of the most effective way to write the scene. Is it best presented through the viewpoint of your protagonist, or someone else in the room?

EXERCISE

Write about the joy and agony of secrets. Write the same scene about the same secret twice, once from the viewpoint of the character telling the information, the other from the viewpoint of the character receiving it. Then, write the scene from the viewpoint of a third character, but assume that they're only able to hear part of what's being said.

THE AGONY OF ALMOST

One thing that makes romantic character relationships so compelling is our natural inclination to be drawn together for companionship and sex. When two intriguing, likable characters are kept apart, whether by choice or circumstance, we empathize with their unfulfilled desires. We've all been there. And to one degree or another, we anticipate—even long for—the moment when their passions are indulged, regardless of logic or taboo. For some readers, these feelings are so strong you might think them masochists, willing to suffer along with the characters they love during their struggle to come together.

Consider adding such layers to your own work, if you're not already doing so. Romance, desire, passion—these can be powerful additions to your writing arsenal, in addition to broadening the scope of your work.

EXERCISE

Practice writing about the moment before two people give into their desires.
In fact, don't let them give in. Use the image at right as your inspiration.
Explore the difficulty of keeping such strong emotions in check.

Violent Intent

From adult literary fiction to children's fantasy novels, violence plays an important role. Make sure that your portrayal of violence is appropriate for the effect you want to achieve. Excitement? Terror? Revulsion? Sorrow? Keep in mind that real violence is not cinematic or exciting. It's ugly. What do you want your reader to feel? In *Hannibal*, Thomas Harris' sequel to *The Silence of the Lambs*, many fans felt the author went too far. They wanted the same terrifying, suspenseful read they got the first time, but instead were treated to a Grande Guignol marathon of gore and gruesomeness, without near the same level of sophistication they found in the previous book.

When composing violent scenes, consider the effect you want to achieve. How do you want your reader to feel after having read the passage? Don't give them what they *don't* want.

EXERCISE

Write about a scene of real violence related to the objects pictured and try to capture the horror, pain, humiliation, and reality of the incident. But challenge yourself. Don't describe any gory specifics. Writing gore is easy—try not doing it.

HOT AND BOTHERED

Unless you're exceptionally good at it, avoid purple prose. It too often devolves into cliché—and not just any cliché, but the kind that starts readers giggling and rolling their eyes. If you're not writing humor, this isn't the response you want.

And you're not writing a *Penthouse* letter (are you?) so if you're going to include a sex scene in your story, try to have it mean something. Is it a cathartic experience for one of the characters? Does it have repercussions later in the story? Is it surprising, depressing, or uplifting? Use it to reveal something about your characters, rather than simply titillate your reader.

Write a sex scene, but without all the thrusting, throbbing clichés that litter so much fiction. With such restrictions, can you still convey the range of emotions you desire?

EXERCISE

Writing as Sculpture

Too often writers fail to produce the amount of material they desire simply because they obsess over the details. The minutia keeps them from achieving the big picture. If that's something you've experienced, consider writing with a different goal in mind.

That's right—put quantity before quality.

Produce as much material as possible without stopping to nitpick over your work. Don't look up words, don't check grammar, or stop to Google the background of a specific reference you want to include in your story. Just write. Once you've finished, you can revise the entire piece with an eye toward specificity of word, rhythm, and content. Like a sculptor or potter, try gathering your raw material first then shape it.

EXERCISE

Write 1,000 words about a potter creating a new piece on her wheel.
Write it quickly and without being overly concerned about the details.
Just produce the work first, then go back and refine it.

CLOAK-AND-DAGGER

Let's focus on a specific genre. You can approach the exercise below in two different ways. You could write your story as a straightforward contemporary spy thriller, or you could set it within the context of a genre you prefer, if it's something other than espionage. In other words, if you write fantasy, your story might be about a spy working for or against a particular sorcerer. If it's romance, make your heroine a spy. Or perhaps she's a normal woman who discovers that her lover is an agent and she gets caught up in his mission. If you prefer literary fiction, raise the stakes on your protagonist's personal issues. Perhaps he's haunted by a moral conflict related to the nature of the duties he's sworn to carry out. Adapt the exercise to whatever genre you prefer: Western, mystery, science fiction, etc.

EXERCISE

Your character senses she's being watched. Out of the corner of her eye she catches sight of a man staring at her. Her mission is to deliver a message to a double agent working for the enemy. Could this man be him, or someone more sinister?

MORE WITH METAPHOR

Per *Merriam Webster's Collegiate Dictionary, Tenth Edition*, metaphor is "a figure of speech in which a word or phrase literally denoting one kind of object or idea is used in place of another to suggest a likeness or analogy between them." As noted, a metaphor is typically limited to a word or phrase (although it may resonate for the entire story). It's a tool designed to quickly convey additional layers of meaning to what's being described.

An interesting exercise, however, is to make your metaphor literal and maintain it for the length of your story. For example, if your protagonist lumbers through life like an elephant, then write him as if he were a literal elephant. This will seem strange at first, but doing so provides you with an enormous amount of insight into what your initial description ("he was like an elephant") really means to the life of your character. You may discover additional character traits that you hadn't considered before.

EXERCISE

Write a story in which your protagonist interviews for a new job. Use the image at left as the basis of your metaphor.

LOOKING AHEAD

In a nutshell, foreshadowing is a writing technique used to hint at an important future event in your story. It's a useful tool. If you want to ratchet up the suspense in your story, foreshadowing a potential danger to your protagonist will do just that. It can also be used to tie a story together thematically. In other words, an idea or conflict (moral, psychological, etc.) hinted at near the beginning of your story becomes an issue the protagonist must eventually face for real.

In *Between the Lines*, Jessica Page Morrell details exactly what can be foreshadowed: 1) set pieces (see p. 159), 2) character transformations, and 3) secrets. When you start any story, determine which of these three possible options will have the biggest impact on your character. Is it the moment at which he figures out how to defeat his antagonist? Is it an unexpected conversation that leads to a life-changing epiphany?

(see p. 159)

EXERCISE

Write a story in which either a set piece, character transformation, or secret is foreshadowed in a scene inspired by the photo at right. When finished, try rewriting the scene, but use it to foreshadow one of the other two choices.

Slow Motion

Time is relative. It slows down or speeds up depending upon our physical and mental responses to the circumstances in which we find ourselves. For example, have you ever been in a car accident, or some other unexpected, near instantaneous experience? In such situations, time sometimes slows to a crawl. You can't do anything about it, but you can see everything that happens as if it's all taking place in slow motion. Details become extraordinarily sharp. Your senses take in the tiniest of details, including background noises, smells, and textures.

Early on in the book *Firewall*, author Andy McNab describes a violent confrontation using this method of slow motion storytelling. Every movement, from planned action to instinctive reaction, is relayed in intense, graphic detail, smoothing out what might be a thirty-second firefight into an extended ballet of violence and suspense.

EXERCISE

Your protagonist drives home during a rainstorm late one night. She takes a sharp corner too quickly and flips her car. She's thrown clear but lands heavily and cannot move. Write this scene and slow down the action wherever you think it will be most effective.

Fast Forward

In the exercise on p. 221 you were asked to write a scene in which time slowed down. In this one, I want you to take the opposite tack. Think about an incident in which you froze. In other words, something happened so quickly that you could neither respond to it in time, nor remember exactly how it happened afterwards.

Complete the exercise detailed at right. Then consider writing the same exercise per the instructions noted on p. 221. Are both manipulations of time effective? Which worked best for the story you were telling? Why? Also, if you wrote the story in third person, consider rewriting it in 1st person. Is conveying the passage of time easier or harder in first person?

EXERCISE

Your protagonist decides to walk his dog one sunny afternoon. We'll call the dog Barnie. Unexpectedly, Barnie gets loose and bolts around the corner of the local coffee shop. The chase is on. Write this scene and pay particular attention to the moment at which the dog first escapes.

Echoes of the Past ❧

The flashback is a fantastic tool. With it, you can reveal the reasons behind a character's motivation or psychology, a secret from their past, or the details of some previous event that help illuminate the "why" and "how" of the main plot. Flashbacks can be a double-edged sword, however. They interrupt your main storyline, bringing to a halt whatever momentum you had going.

Is the tradeoff worth it? It certainly can be, but keep in mind the following rule: The length of your flashback should be relative to the importance of the information revealed. For example, if your protagonist fondly remembers swimming in the local creek as a child, keep it short—a few lines or a paragraph at most. If, however, she witnessed a friend drown in that very same creek, and the details of their relationship and the event itself are critical to understanding her actions in the present, the flashback can be much longer—even multiple chapters.

EXERCISE

The woman at left is on her way to meet someone from her past. She's nervous about it. Create a flashback that illuminates the nature of their relationship and why it causes her such anxiety.

What's Your Point of View?

In *A Game of Thrones* and subsequent volumes of the epic fantasy series *A Song of Fire and Ice*, George R.R. Martin crafts an enormous tale in which multiple viewpoints are used throughout. Using each member of his extremely large cast of characters, Martin shows readers the same events from different points of view, reveals critical information through unexpected means, and provides a more objective, surprising narrative for having done so.

Martin's tale is extraordinarily complex, making his use of multiple viewpoints seem more daunting than perhaps it really is. In a simpler tale, multiple viewpoints can be a fresh, fun way to add new dimensions to your storytelling.

EXERCISE

Write a story about a young clerk working at the store pictured. In the security mirror, he sees a woman stuffing an expensive piece of merchandise into her coat. Begin writing the scene from the clerk's viewpoint. At some point, continue the story from the woman's viewpoint. Consider adding a third viewpoint when a police officer or some other character takes notice of the scene.

COMBAT FATIGUE

Some days, writing is just plain hard, like being in a long, extended battle. At the end of the day, you're worn out and sick of writing, hoping that the next time will be easier. But it's always going to be a bit of a fight.

Consider this book your field medic, someone who can patch you up and provide relief from the daily grind. Writing prompts allow you to stop worrying about larger projects and focus on short, relatively simple assignments. Compose a two-page short story. Write a six-line poem. It doesn't matter what so long as you keep coming back for more. That's what wins the war. Eventually your inspiration will return, you'll feel rested, and you'll *want* to tackle that big project.

EXERCISE

When you get tired of a story you're working on, write a short scene in which the protagonist from the story attempts to cook dinner for friends. That's right—even if your character is a badass Navy Seal, he's got to eat. There's no pressure to create anything lengthy or complex. Have fun with it. Re-engage with the character in this unexpected situation, and think about the qualities that inspired you to create him in the first place.

DATE 20NOV

FLIGHT
DL427

DL427
CINCINNATI

DESTINATION
SEATTLE

OPERATED BY DELTA AIR

DL240

20N

THE BIG REVEAL

The surprise ending. The plot twist. When these are well done, they can be wonderful fun. Consider *The Sixth Sense* and *The Usual Suspects*. Or from literature, Dan Brown's *The Da Vinci Code,* Chuck Palahniuk's *Fight Club,* or Patrick Süskind's *Perfume: The Story of a Murderer.*

And yet, as enjoyable as such twists can be, they can pose a danger to writers who don't know what they're doing. If predictable, pedestrian, or illogical, the surprise can mar every part of the story that preceded it. Your audience has spent their money and time in good faith. Fail to deliver, or deliver badly, and their disappointment can be extreme. Still, adding an unforeseen turn of events to your story can be a blast. It just takes practice. Try your hand at the one detailed below.

EXERCISE

Your protagonist's supervisor orders him to call on a newly acquired client out of state. What your protagonist doesn't know is that something about this meeting is a set up— the location, the client, maybe even the meeting itself. Who's behind it and why? Keep both your protagonist and your reader unaware of what's really going on until "the big reveal."

MULTIPLE MENTORS

Few things will benefit you more than a good mentor. If you're lucky, this may be a teacher or a more experienced writer. For many of us, however, our mentors are the authors we read.

If you believe that certain authors are particularly good, and that you can learn by studying how they write, do so. Keep in mind, however, that just because you like a particular author doesn't mean that he excels at all aspects of the craft. Make sure you're aware of what his strengths are. Robert Louis Stevenson's are plot and structure. Nick Hornby's is characterization. Elmore Leonard's is dialogue. No author is good at everything in equal measure. Recognize that fact and learn from the people who excel at specific things. Also, learn what your own strengths are. Then, when you write, do two things: Rely on your strengths, but work to improve your weaknesses.

Here There Be Dragons

"Here There Be Dragons" was used on ancient European maps to indicate areas that were unexplored, possibly dangerous. Think of your story as a map. Your protagonist is traveling (whether physically or metaphorically) towards an unknowable final conflict. If her goals are to be achieved, the conflict is unavoidable. Maybe she needs to overcome her inflexible pride to win the love of a man. Or sneak into a secure military facility to liberate a captive alien being.

Your understanding of what that great unknown is clarifies as you write your way toward it. You may know what you'd like to have happen, but you haven't yet determined all of the specifics. If so, consider writing the climax first, filling in that part of the map ahead of time.

EXERCISE

The location pictured is home to your climax—where the "dragon" lives. Here, your protagonist and his son will have one final confrontation that resolves their long-standing enmity. Flesh out the details of the scene first, then write the story leading up to it. Does knowing about the climax in advance make the journey to it easier?

IT'S GOOD TO BE BAD

The best way to ensure that your protagonist faces a challenge worthy of your readers' time is to create an antagonist who is her equal (good) or superior (better). For example, Lady de Winter is more than a match for D'Artagnan. And only Professor Moriarty could challenge Sherlock Holmes. Jack Ryan had Marko Ramius. And, of course, Captain Ahab had his whale.

If the opposition doesn't measure up, your protagonist is diminished. Consider the stories you've already written based on the prompts within this book. In each case, was the opposition to your protagonist equal to or better than him? Find an example where the antagonist could be improved and rewrite the story keeping those improvements in mind. Is your story more effective? More exciting? Is the danger to your protagonist (in whatever form it takes) more pronounced?

EXERCISE

Your hero is a young squire who yearns to become a knight. While on the field of battle, the knight to whom he attends is killed by another man-at-arms. The squire, in a fit of rage, charges onto the battlefield, dagger in hand. What happens next? Remember—your squire is terribly overmatched.

MODUS OPERANDI

Many writers are more comfortable writing with a particular point of view. They also have a preferred location in which to write, as well as a preferred time of day. This is sensible. There's some benefit, however, to changing your routine. Routine can lead to stagnation and boredom. Be willing to try things differently every once in a while. Write outside. Write after dinner rather than first thing in the morning. Write in a coffee shop and let the buzz of other people energize you.

Your protagonist returns to the parking garage where she left her car, only to find it missing. It's late at night, she has no cell phone, and there are no taxis. Write about her efforts to get home from first or third person point of view, whichever you're most comfortable with. Then, rewrite the story from the point of view you did not use. Did your story change? Did the exercise enable you to come up with additional ideas about your character and her situation?

Red Shirts

I like *Star Trek* as much as the next person. That said I also appreciate the humor of the "red shirt" dilemma. If you're unfamiliar with it, let me explain. *Star Trek* was notorious for including a few nameless crew members in each landing party. They always wore red shirts (I don't know why) and were good for only one thing—getting killed. It happened so often that a red shirt became synonymous with "death wish."

It also became comical. Keep that in mind. Readers won't get worked up over a character's death if you don't provide him with any interesting, sympathetic, or endearing qualities. Readers have no empathy for such characters. Their deaths have no impact.

Consider *Jaws*. The first person to die is on screen for perhaps sixty seconds. But in the few moments we see her alive, she's with her lover, enjoying life. We know that someone cares for her—that they'll be devastated when she turns up missing. We feel bad when she dies, alone and terrified. No Red Shirt ever had such moments.

EXERCISE

Write a story in which a group of strangers get lost in the environment pictured. One of them dies early on, indicating just how dangerous their situation is. Provide this character with enough moments of humanity to ensure that his passing has some impact.

CHAPTER EIGHT

UNLIMITED POTENTIAL

> "Twice and thrice over, as they say, good is it to repeat and review what is good." —PLATO

This chapter is devoted to providing you with new ways to think about the images in the preceding pages—suggestions for using them a second time, or even a third, without repeating any of the story elements you initially developed.

It's my hope that you get multiple uses out of these images. Doing so will not only make the book infinitely more valuable, but it will force you to become even more creative, clever, and willing to experiment with your fiction.

What's Not There

When using images to help create characters and stories, consider what you're not seeing as well as what you are. Take, for example, the picture at left. How do this man's body language, expression, and situation relate to what's *not* made explicit in the photo?

He appears somewhat annoyed, so perhaps he had a bad day at work. Maybe a job offer fell through, or he failed to salvage an important relationship. There's no obvious reason for him to be alone, so perhaps he's waiting for someone. If so, who? Is he looking forward to the meeting? If not, why? Might one of the circumstances noted above, or something similarly distressing, be one of the reasons?

EXERCISE

Once you've figured out what's preoccupying our protagonist, think about how such things affect his ability to respond to other people and situations. Then, write at least 1,000 words detailing a meeting between him and another character. This character should not have anything to do with what's on the man's mind. Instead, use what's on his mind to shape how he interacts with the character. Look back over the other photos in this book and consider what's not there.

The Woman in the Window

In 1945, Fritz Lang directed the film noir classic *The Woman in the Window*. The tagline for the film was "It was the look in her eyes that made him think of murder." When I first saw the image at right, it made me think of both Lang's film and Hitchcock's legendary *Psycho*. I imagined Norman Bates' mother, looking down upon her latest guest/victim, backlit by the dusty yellow lights of her cobweb-shrouded bedroom. My first instinct, then, was to write about something mysterious or macabre. First instincts, however, are not always the best source for story ideas.

EXERCISE

Write the story of this woman, but only after having taken a closer look at the photo. Notice that her figure is actually that of a shadow cast upon a wooden floor. We are in the room with her, rather than outside looking in. Notice the rounded shape of her belly. Perhaps she's pregnant. What might she be contemplating and why? Is she happy or melancholy? Is she looking out the window, or standing with her back to it? How does this difference change the nature of your story? Take a second look at the other photos in this book and see if you can spot details that spark new story ideas.

Freedom

Allow yourself the freedom to experiment with fiction. Consider: Do you limit your storytelling choices by assuming that certain stories must be told in certain ways, or with certain types of characters? Do you restrict your creativity in order to ensure work that appeals to the widest possible audience?

Take the picture at left. What kind of story might this image inspire? Would you write about the pig, or the people who own her? If you focus your story on the pig, would you tell it from her point of view? Outside of children's fiction, such as E.B. White's *Charlotte's Web*, would readers take such a story seriously?

Be daring in your choices. A story about pigs can be as powerful as any other work of art. George Orwell's *Animal Farm* is an obvious example, but clearly shows that artistry is in the telling, not the tale.

EXERCISE

Write a story about the day this pig decides to flee the farm. It can be serious or humorous. Consider the other images in this book. Find one that inspired you to write a new story, but allow yourself the freedom to use whatever setting, characters, points of view, or structure you like, even if your choices seem absurd or limiting.

Extend the life of this book by going back and re-using the images you've already written about. The method detailed below is both challenging and fun. Here's how it works: Flip through the book and select an image at random. Then roll one six-sided dice. The number rolled corresponds to an exercise in the list below. Using the randomly selected photo as your inspiration, complete the assignment. Be sure to write at least 1,000 words.

MIX AND MATCH

Pick a photo. Roll the die. Write your story. If you want, you can start with the image at left.
1) The subject of the photo compels your protagonist to run for his life.
2) Your protagonist has a dramatic history with the subject of the photo. What is it?
3) The photo represents where your story ends. It begins with a door slamming.
4) The photo represents where your story begins. It ends with a kiss.
5) The subject of the photo is not what it seems. Write the true story.
6) Your protagonist encounters the subject of the photo. The event changes her life.

> Suppose someone has frequently flown
> in his dreams and finally becomes conscious
> of a power and an art of flying....

—FRIEDRICH NIETZSCHE

There are plenty of books available devoted to helping writers find ideas. One of the best is *The Writer's Idea Book* by Jack Heffron. Resources such as these will, to one degree or another, facilitate the process of generating stories. However, while most suggest looking for ideas in newspapers, memories, articles, and overheard conversations, few, if any, focus specifically upon photos and other imagery. They're missing out.

Consider all the work you've done with the prompts in this book so far. All of the ways in which you've been told to think about images and look for visual cues that might lead to potential stories. It follows that any good magazine can provide enough ideas to keep you busy for weeks. Look at everything from advertisements to features. Anything with a picture. It works, and you'll never be at a loss for a good story idea if you simply open your mind to the possibilities.

Let me tell you one final story that takes this idea an extra step. Several months ago, I took my first drawing course at the local art academy. The instructor related to us that after having worked with perspective for so long, she found that every time she looked down a street, at a building, or even at a group of people, she couldn't *not* see the lines of perspective that ran through the scene. It became instinctual, as if her mind had become so conditioned to thinking about such things that it automatically translated whatever she saw into the language of art. I honestly believe that images can work the same way for writers. No matter where you are, no matter what you're looking at, ideas—good ideas—are abundant. Every room you walk into, conversation you have, and dream you imagine becomes a wellspring of story.

Open your eyes.
The ideas are right there in front of you.

ABOUT THE AUTHOR

Phillip Sexton

Phillip Sexton is one of the founders and editors of *Fresh Boiled Peanuts*, a literary journal. He is also a co-author of *The Writer's Book of Matches: 1001 Prompts to Ignite Your Fiction* and has published a wide range of articles and essays. He lives in Cincinnati, Ohio, where he is currently at work on his next book, *Legends of Literature*.

Thanks to the following people: my partner in crime Tricia Bateman, for creating such a beautiful piece of art (and for all the heavy lifting that most people will never know about); Amy Schell, our exceptional editor, for her invaluable insights and advice; my good friends at *Fresh Boiled Peanuts*, Alice, Amy, Scott, Steve, and Suzanne, for their support and good humor; Jane Friedman, for seeing this project's potential in the first place; Cindy, Mike, and Jennifer for faith; and Claudean, Grace, Kelly, and Michelle, good friends all at Writer's Digest Books.

Tricia Bateman

After a decade as an award-winning graphic designer, Tricia shares her first photographs for publication with *A Picture Is Worth 1,000 Words*. Her exposure to design came early through her father's own career as a designer and for the last ten years, she has been designing for a variety of publications and is currently the senior art director at *HOW* magazine.

Almost everyone I know has lent a hand, a foot, or a partial profile to the photos in this book. They are too numerous to mention individually, but I am grateful to every one of them. Thanks to: Phil for trusting me with his idea and being unflappable during this process; Claudean Wheeler and Amy Schell for patiently answering months of questions; the *HOW* staff for patience and encouragement during production; Hal Barkan for quality control on the photos; Tracy Jackson for saving what would have been a lost weekend; Jim Krause for reminding me how fun photography is; Suzanne, Michelle, Nick, Jeff, and Melanie for their sustaining friendship.

FURTHER READING

Characters & Viewpoint
Orson Scott Card
WRITER'S DIGEST BOOKS, 1998

Finding Your Voice
Les Edgerton
WRITER'S DIGEST BOOKS, 2003

Screenplay
Syd Field
DELL, 1984

Writing Fiction
Gotham Writers' Workshop
BLOOMSBURY USA, 2003

Write Great Fiction: Dialogue
Gloria Kempton
WRITER'S DIGEST BOOKS, 2004

On Writing
Stephen King
SCRIBNER, 2000

The 3 A.M. Epiphany
Brian Kiteley
WRITER'S DIGEST BOOKS, 2005

The Modern Library Writer's Workshop
Stephen Koch
MODERN LIBRARY, 2003

Beginnings, Middles & Ends
Nancy Kress
WRITER'S DIGEST BOOKS, 1999

Word Painting
Rebecca McClanahan
WRITER'S DIGEST BOOKS, 2000

Story
Robert McKee
REGAN BOOKS, 1997

Between the Lines
Jessica Page Morrell
WRITER'S DIGEST BOOKS, 2006

Fiction Writer's Workshop
Josip Novakovich
STORY PRESS, 1998

Story Structure Architect
Victoria Lynn Schmidt, Ph.D.
WRITER'S DIGEST BOOKS, 2005

Stein on Writing
Sol Stein
ST. MARTIN'S GRIFFIN, 2000

20 Master Plots
Ronald B. Tobias
WRITER'S DIGEST BOOKS, 2003

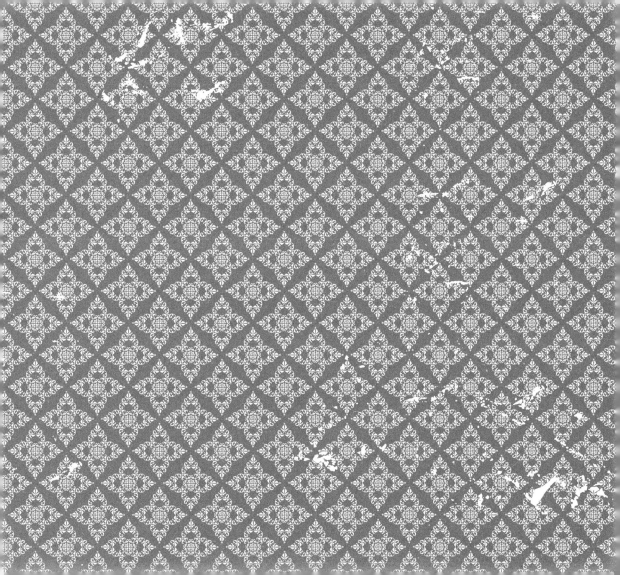